AN ILLUSTRATED HISTORY OF

Traction Engines

Garrett Tractor used for light haulage.

PETER WILKES

An Illustrated History of

TRACTION

ENGINES

SPURBOOKS LIMITED

PUBLISHED BY
SPURBOOKS LTD
6 PARADE COURT
BOURNE END
BUCKINGHAMSHIRE

First published 1974
Reprinted 1979

ISBN 0 904978 46 X

Printed in Great Britain by
McCorquodale (Newton) Ltd., Newton-le-Willows, Lancashire.

Contents

Illustrations

CHAPTER I

Come to the Rally

The Traction Engine Rally is now an established part of the summer scene. Every year, from early April through to August and beyond, people by the thousand spend at least part of their weekend in the open countryside where these giants from a past engineering age gather. Some meetings are small, a mere handful of engines adding to the attraction of village carnival or fête. Others, such as the newly introduced "Expo Steam" of the "Harwood House Rally and Old Time Fair", attract up to a hundred or more engines from Europe as well as the British Isles. Frequently meetings will be extended to show the traction engines working under identical conditions to those familiar in the heyday of steam, a period which lasted from the late 1890's to the 1920's.

Whatever kind of meeting, traction engines guarantee to draw enthusiastic crowds. What is the cause of this enthusiasm for machines that at one time we willingly allowed to rot away into oblivion, disinterested in their future, unconcerned with their past?. Partly, of course, it is a trait in the British character. For how often have we failed to appreciate something until it is on the verge of extinction? This, in itself, cannot be the complete answer. For there are other reminders of a past age which, while drawing enthusiasm from the specialist or expert, fail to move the ordinary man in the way that the traction engine does.

The true reasons for this revival of interest in machines that played such a part in the development of the economic wealth of the country are many and varied. To some it is the fascination of a vanished age; the ability to see once again a way of life that has been lost forever. Some get pleasure from viewing at first hand a standard of engineering that is rarely equalled and never bettered in this age of mass production. Others love the gleaming brass and shining paintwork of the Showman's Road Locomotive, and remember or imagine the days when, on village green or city square, the air was heavy with smoke, and the individual smell of steam assailed the nostrils to announce, again, that the fair had arrived, to bring pleasure to young and old.

No one can visit such a gathering of engines and come away disappointed. The organisers go to considerable lengths to ensure that the meeting is truly a family occasion, with something to interest all. Obviously the machines themselves are the stars, and Traction Engine Rallies, unlike other events, give the public a chance to identify themselves with the engines and their crews. Far from remaining onlookers, they can enter fully into the spirit of the occasion and participate in the many events that give them the chance to try their hand as "engine drivers".

As the Rallies began to attract the public in ever increasing numbers, so those responsible sought ways to draw onlookers actively into the events and the steam traction engine is eminently suitable for public participation. A mere collection of engines would have been only of passing interest. No other road machine travels so slowly, giving the uninitiated the time to correct errors that may occur in their handling. Hence, providing a qualified engine man was on board to concern himself with the state of the fire and water

A parade of pride – a 1913 Aveling Porter steam tractor leads the parade.

pressure and generally be in charge of the controls, the steering could be left to someone who possibly had never before climbed on to the "footplate".

The Rally Catalogue clearly shows the chances that exist for the visitor to prove his skill, or lack of it, against other similar fortunates. Every meeting begins with the Grand Parade. The engines seem galvanised into action as one after another they make their way into the arena, to be described by the commentator. Then, after a period when photographers are allowed into the ring to record the beauty and magnificence on film, the events of the day begin. First may come musical chairs. Volunteer steersmen from the crowd join each engine driver, and soon they are under way. The steersman, learning his art the hard way, tries, often in vain, to keep the wheels pointing in the direction intended. As the music stops so do the engines, and steersman or woman now becomes runner, as he or she races for one of the petrol or oil drums encircling the arena.

Gradually the number of drums and engines decreases until there is but

The glory of Traction Engine Rallies is the chance that one gets to participate in the actual events. Here the author acts as steersman on the 1927 Foster engine.

one drum for two engines. Tension mounts as each tries to keep his engine closest to it, and the music seems to go on forever. Then the moment of truth. The two steersmen race for the one drum. One, the victor, the other the vanquished, but each has learned the thrill that can only come to someone fortunate enough to be actively involved in working one of the various classes of traction engine.

The chance to become acquainted with the engines is not confined to the ring events. The steam fraternity is one of the most friendly in the country, and there can be few engine owners who will not go to great lengths to explain everything about their own particular engine and its workings to whoever shows interest. Nor do they expect a high technical knowledge. An interest in these machines of the past is all that is needed for the "experts" to pass on their knowledge.

Even the ring events have their rivals at most meetings. For "traction engine" is synonymous with "fair ground" and whatever the size of the meeting the fair will usually be present. Here amusements and rides of long ago are brought to life, more often than not powered by those great Showman's Locomotives which attracted such attention during their working days. Again they stand in all their glory, the generator at the front providing power not only for the amusement or ride, but for the coloured lights that hang from their canopies, to provide, as dusk falls, a picture that mere words cannot describe.

Yet there is one pleasant intrusion into the world of these giants, and that is the work of the model maker. Here perfect traction engines in miniature add yet another attraction for those who make it part of their weekend pleasure to visit a Traction Engine Rally.

Truly these meetings have something for every member of the family, and every section of the community. Yet, but for one man, the Traction Engine Rally may never have come into being, and without doubt our present would be the poorer for its omission.

Arthur Napper is identical with most traction engine owners, in having a great inbuilt pride in his engine. No true steam enthusiast will ever admit that his machine may be second best to any other. Hence, when Arthur Napper and his close friend Miles Chetwynd-Stapylton came together, their conversation turned to steam – to traction engines in general, and their own engines in particular. To Arthur Napper nothing could equal "Old Timer", his 1902 Marshall general purpose engine; not even the magnificently restored 1918 Aveling engine, "Lady Grove", proudly owned by Mr. Chetwynd-Stapylton. Hence, as the merits of the two engines were argued, a wager was struck. For a firkin of beer the two would again raise steam in anger, and race against each other over a measured course on Arthur Napper's farm at Appleton, Berkshire.

News of the meeting spread, and on that summer afternoon in 1950 a small crowd gathered to see again a form of transport that seemed in danger of dying out. But even they could hardly have realised that history was being made before their eyes. Arthur Napper himself then had little idea of the forces of enthusiasm that were to be released that afternoon. Yet as the machines lined up for the start the two men found themselves caught up in the fervour of public excitement. Acclaim for the two engines was loud and long. Then, as "Old Timer" began to draw away from its rival, the cheering reached a crescendo as the onlookers urged it to victory. As his engine breasted the tape ahead of the Aveling, an idea was formed in Arthur Napper's mind that has given us the Traction Engine Rally as we know it today.

Progress in the first place was slow. Napper himself carried the idea forward when he organised what could be claimed as the first ever traction engine rally at his own farm. It is an interesting fact that this, the birthplace of the movement, has never since been without its annual rally.

Gradually the idea spread. In other regions enthusiasts organised meetings of locally owned engines. More important, bodies sprang up to co-operate the work of these people, and so give a solid foundation on which the rally movement was able to build.

Although we owe an obvious debt of gratitude to Arthur Napper, we owe an equal debt to the men who so unselfishly restore these engines to their former state of glory and bring them, often considerable distances at great expense, in order that we may share in their beauty and magnificence. Today traction engines are no longer cheap items either to buy, restore or maintain. Immediately after World War II, when the countryside was littered with the remains of these unwanted "work horses of steam", it was possible to pick one up for the scrap value.

Indeed, such was the minimal value placed on them in 1947 that a splendid Showman's Road Locomotive was sold for only £25. This was the price paid for "Victory", a 1920 8 n.h.p. double crank compound engine No. 3827, which had been built by Charles Burrell of Thetford, for Charles Thurston of Norwich, and was used on fairgrounds throughout eastern England. Today, if sold, it would fetch more than two hundred times that amount.

Similarly, at a time when agriculture was saying a sad farewell to steam cultivation, a matched pair of massive Fowler ploughing engines could be easily obtained for £100. Recently two such engines, one in working order and the other needing repair, were advertised for sale with offers requested in the region of £5,000

Nor is a desire to own, a certainty that ownership will come about. The sad fact is that there are far too few traction engines of any type laying about waiting to be discovered. Most of those which survived the breaker's hammer,

*A 1913 Marshall, No. 61880, used up to the end of World War II.
It was restored in 1955*

during the period when hardly anyone could see a future use for them, have passed into the hands of loving and caring owners. To suggest to most steam men that they part with their engine is like asking them to give up part of life itself, so the availability of engines is indeed short.

To the owner, upkeep can be considerable. Even the engineering standards of those great days cannot last forever. Age causes fireboxes to become thinner, until the time comes when replacement can no longer be postponed. This one job alone can cost up to £500. Steam engines, above all other vehicles, require regular safety checks. A boiler explosion, as well as wrecking a fine example of some particular engine, could so easily cause the death or serious injury of innocent bystanders. For this reason insurance is compulsory, and cover is only granted when an Inspector of the Insurance Company is satisfied that the machine is, in every respect, roadworthy and safe.

Unlike many hobbyists, the traction engine owner has no chance to recover his costs by means of awards and prizes. True, appearance money is given for

1910 Robey 6 h.p. compound traction engine No. 29930

*Final touches being applied to a 1910 Robey tractor
at the Carrington Park Rally, Lincolnshire*

each meeting attended, together with free coal, but this is little return for a man who may have brought his expensive engine hundreds of miles on a low loader.

The person, however, who develops an enthusiasm for steam, but is unable either to afford or discover his own engine, has no need to despair. The movement will welcome him with open arms. There are Traction Engine Clubs in most areas, and ownership of an engine is not a necessity for membership. Anyone with a desire to help in preservation work can be assured of a warm greeting. For, among other things, when heavy restoration work has to be carried out, most owners are only too pleased with a sincere offer of help from a local person known to be keen and interested in the job.

There are no less than thirty-six local clubs throughout England, Scotland, Wales and Ireland. In addition, the National Traction Engine Club, formed in 1954 with, appropriately enough, Arthur Napper as President, is open to all.

This club not only acts as the governing body for the rally movement, but

1911 Fowler General Purpose engine, No. 12761, used by Forestry Commission for work on private roads

produces a most interesting magazine for members, devoted to both the traction engines themselves and the men who spent their working life amidst the smell of oil and smoke. Reading accounts of a "life in steam" can only bring one closer to those who today spend their spare time and, in many respects, their lives, making sure that traction engines are never forgotten.

Neither is the specialist overlooked. The man or woman who develops a love for one particular type of engine is also catered for. The Steam Plough Club is one example in this direction. Here those enthusiasts who have done so much to preserve and even perfect the art of steam ploughing, and acquired the knowledge to demonstrate the methods to the public, invite anyone with a similar love for these massive engines to join their ranks.

There is no feeling of isolation among members living in various parts of the country. Wherever steam cultivating is demonstrated, some at least of those who make up the Steam Plough Club will gather, to talk, to admire, but above all else to commentate and describe to those watching, every aspect of this method of land cultivation.

The Rally movement is, indeed, all embracing. Here is something for

1917 Mann's Steam Tractor, designed for direct ploughing work and road haulage. An example of what the expert can do to provide an engine for his own requirements. It now has a front dynamo fitted to power the owner's Fair Organ

everyone, from the relaxation and pleasure gained from the mere presence of these old timers, to the time given in researching their history and helping to preserve them.

My own interest in traction engines and the men who used them developed from a life-long love of the countryside, and the people who live and work in it. Through them I have spent many happy hours listening to stories of days gone by, and marvelling at the way farm labourers, as they were so erroneously called, for who is more skilled than the man who can turn his hand from ploughing to reaping, from hedging to threshing, accepted a way of life that saw hard work but very little play. The traction engine brought the beginnings of relief from this bondage.

It is my sincere hope that in the pages that follow I can share my own enthusiasm for the men and machines which started a revolution in the countryside and followed it through, against the die-hard prejudices of those horse loving men then in authority, until the traction engine, in all its various forms, became a familiar and loved sight in both towns and villages.

1930 Aveling and Porter Roller. Originally restored as a Roller, it has now been further converted to a Showman's type tractor and mounted on pneumatic tyres

forms, became a familiar and loved sight in both towns and villages.

The book does not intend to be a technical treatise on these old steamers. Rather it tries to show the evolution of steam; of men who had the foresight to see steam power harnessed for the good of the nation.

In layout it follows the pattern adopted by most rally catalogues, and the value of these can never be underestimated. Many are beautifully prepared booklets that add greatly to one's enjoyment, with their snippets of information about the entries and owners past and present. Even more important, for the visitor, catalogues are arranged to show the various classes.

Although many engines may look alike, all fall into distinct classes depending on the work they were required to do. The traction engine evolved in a distinct fashion, starting on the farm and progressing to use in heavy haulage throughout the country. Opposition was strong, laws were often harsh towards the unfortunate engine driver and owner. Yet inevitably change came, and as each change in conditions arrived, so the engine makers were ready with yet another type to meet the new demand. Each class, then, tells of some aspect of the struggle to overcome opposition, and the eventual success which saw steam reign supreme on land and road in Great Britain for over a quarter of a century.

CHAPTER II

Steam Comes to the Farm

There is nothing new under the sun. Time and again the truth of that statement is brought home to us and nowhere is this more so than in the country. The combine harvester, so often thought of as the ultimate of the modern mind, had a competitor in the times when the bullock was the beast of burden. Although impracticable on account of the thirty or more such beasts required for motive power, it does show that so often modern design is but the furtherance of ancient thoughts.

Today, one of the most up-to-date machines offered to the farmer proudly boasts of a unique cup action – precisely the same action which was in common use in the early years of the century. This maxim applied also to steam. Although, to the 19th century pioneers, the traction engine was the product of their own minds, the use of steam, as motive power, had been known in pre-Christian times, when Hero of Alexandria is said to have made an engine powered by that medium. However, there is no need to go back so far in history, other than to recall that, in every age, man has searched for progress. The early engines were of such weird design that they bore little resemblance to the traction engine of the early days.

Development, however, followed a logical path. As early as 1618, David Ramsey obtained a patent to "plough and work an impliment of agriculture without the use of either oxen or beast". The idea in Ramsey's mind has been lost in the pages of history. Whether he did, in fact, experiment with any form or device to improve the lot of those working the soil by time honoured, laboured and inefficient methods, we can only surmise, but what is not in doubt, is that it was his intention to harness steam for the good of the countryside.

For the modern Rally enthusiast, however, steam can be said to have had its beginnings in the remarkable achievements of Richard Trevithick, at the turn of the 19th century. In many ways this Cornishman could lay claim to the title, "Father of Steam". It was he who released designers from the inherent disability of Watt's low pressure engine and boiler, with its huge cylinder and piston, and gave them the modern high pressure engine, which, although smaller, was capable of developing similar power.

Trevithick, of course, like most early steam pioneers, was concerned with the use of steam as motive power. His first efforts were shown on Christmas Eve, 1801, in the form of a road vehicle designed to carry seven passengers. And, according to one chronicler of the age, the carriage ascended Camborne Beacon, in West Cornwall, "like a bird". Successful in other trials, Trevithick was granted a patent for the invention and in the following year, with his partner Vivian, he built a carriage for use in London.

Unwieldly by modern standards, with a wrought iron boiler and cylinder enclosed in the horizontal position, it had the distinction of working. The piston was connected, through a con rod, to two gears which drove the ten foot diameter rear wheels. The carriage itself, capable of carrying ten people, was mounted on great springs and gave a remarkably comfortable ride. The designer, however, could not overcome public prejudice. Here, to the general public, and indeed to most in authority, was a frightening, belching monster such as had never been seen before. It is said that many, seeing it for the first time, ran away in terror. In sympathy with people of the age, who knew nothing of the world other than the small piece of it in which they lived, the sight of Trevithick's strange contraption must indeed have been a frightening sight. Small wonder that, when his initial financial backing ran out he was unable to obtain more. The coach, sadly, was removed from its mountings, and the engine ended its working life in a mill.

Trevithick now turned his back on steam road vehicles, and threw most of his energy into the development of the steam railway. It was to the latter's benefit and the former's loss. Yet despite his setbacks and disappointments, he never completely forgot those early ideas. By 1812 he was advertising portable steam engines for use in threshing and grinding corn, sawing wood and other agricultural tasks. The engines, weighing 15 cwts, were priced at £63.

The climate of opinion, however, was against the introduction of such engines. The country was in a disturbed state. Grain prices were high, with a subsequent drop in demand. Farmers as a whole were cash conscious, and although some large landowners bought Trevithick's portable, and found it lived up to all his claims, the smaller farmer was not prepared to spend money on an engine when he felt unsure that it would improve his lot. So, for a period of some twenty years, the portable engine stagnated. Many who, in other circumstances would have turned their attentions to this new development in the field of agriculture, let the opportunity pass.

Progress, however, be it in the Dark Ages, or our own modern technological times, cannot be denied. By 1830, Nathan Gough, from Salford, Lancashire was talking of producing an even better portable engine for use

The popularity of the Portable is shown by this Foster,
made in 1942 to satisfy a still existing demand

wherever motive power was required. Unfortunately Gough is another of the many who left no records. Today we are unable to say if his theory turned into reality or if his ideas were but pipe dreams. Yet it was an indication of the wind of change that was now blowing through the agricultural world. The market was more stable and those who, a few years ago, had held back from manufacture, now turned their attention to the improvement of the early portable engines, such as those by Trevithick.

One of the most remarkable of all who were concerned in the portable was a man called Howden. At the 1839 Agricultural Show, held at Wrangle in Lincolnshire, he both astounded and delighted the farmers present with an impressive portable engine.

Small, in comparison with others of the age, it produced adequate power for use on the farm and, from test reports, was of proven reliability. Here, many farmers saw the answer to their needs. Howden himself was not impressed with this public acclaim. Manufacture, he said, must be kept at a low level otherwise his engines would flood the market, the countryside

Steam at work on the farm. A reconstruction of steam threshing

would be overstocked and their maker face ruin. Fortune evaded him due solely to this short sighted outlook. For while he turned his attentions elsewhere, others followed his example, and by the end of the 19th century were turning out portable engines as fast as possible. The countryside, now eager and demanding, had absorbed no less than thirty thousand working engines by that time.

For poor Howden it was too late. He had made his decision and had to stick to it. He had the ability, but not the faith. While others prospered, he could only look on. Within two years of Howden's erroneous thoughts, a name that was to echo through the corridors of steam presented to the public a portable engine designed for the agriculturalist. Ransomes of Ipswich had arrived on the scene.

The founder was Robert Ransome, who was born in 1753, the son of a Norfolk schoolmaster. After completing his education he was apprenticed to an ironmonger in Norwich. His choice of career was a wise one, for soon he had opened his own business and acquired a small iron foundry. This fired his imagination, and experimental work led to him being granted a patent for tempering plough shares, then made from cast iron. Soon expansion became necessary, and the now famous connection with the town of Ipswich began. The work undertaken by the firm was varied. Not only did Ransome build agricultural implements, but they constructed the second Stoke Bridge, and built and installed Ipswich's gasometer and the pipes necessary for the town's supply. Although the founder died in 1830, the firm had been built on solid foundations, and work increased and multiplied. Steam however was to prove their true excellence. By 1841 Ransome's first portable engine was exhibited at the Royal Show at Liverpool. It was, although few of those attending could have realised it, an historic moment. Ransome had ideas that could have seen a much earlier birth of the traction engine as we know it today.

The Royal Show in 1842 was held at Bristol, and those who made for the Ransome exhibit were not disappointed. Last year's portable was this year's self propelled. Now the farmer had the chance to buy a completely new type of machine. A sprocket fitted to the engine shaft drove a larger sprocket on one of the rear wheels. Also the chassis had been lengthened to accommodate a small threshing machine. Here seemed the complete agricultural investment. Reports were enthusiastic. The power developed exceeded 5 h.p., with an hourly intake of 36 gallons of water and 50lbs of coke. Despite the fact that a horse was needed between the shafts for steerage, it earned the top award of £300.

Alas, to no avail. The farmers themselves had no inclination to buy. Perhaps it was the fact that the purchaser had to take the threshing drum as well as the engine; perhaps it was die-hard attitudes that refused to accept self propulsion, preferring the engine they knew. Whatever the reasons, Ransome's valiant attempt to modernise the portable had failed. Sadly the threshing drum was removed and engine and drum sold separately.

After this failure, manufacturers could have been forgiven if they had accepted the old time prejudices in favour of time honoured methods, and turned their attentions to other things. Fortunately the inventor and designer is a creature of perseverance. Portables continued to appear and Ransome's, at least, was not too discouraged. The design team was already thinking far ahead, and the company continued to exhibit its designs at agricultural shows.

Today, such a show is a chance for townsfolk and country people to meet on common ground. The townsman can see and examine not only the latest in agricultural machinery, but also crafts that were at one time in danger of dying out. It brings entertainment for every sector of the community. Agricultural Shows are the only outdoor meetings to rival Traction Engine Rallies as a form of popular leisure activity.

However, at the time when the portable engine was fighting to establish a stronghold in the countryside, things were different. Then each village was, in most ways, an isolated community, each dependent on the other for its well being. Transport, other than the horse, was unknown. Travel, except for the favoured few, was something that villagers rarely considered, especially over long distances.

Each community would have representation of trades. There would be the grocer, the butcher, and the publican, more often than not brewing his own beer. There would also be an undertaker, milliner, shoe maker and saddle maker. For the farmer, the largest employer of labour, there would be the blacksmith and wheelwright. The joiner would have premises, as would the baker, mason and draper. In larger villages there could be more than one person engaged in the same trade, and often a man would have two trades. The innkeeper would often carry on business as a harness maker or wheelwright. This then was the background of the countryside that the engine maker sought to infiltrate.

Today advertising is easy, through the medium of the newspaper, trade publications and television. Then it was far from easy. Many influential land owners and farmers, the men concerned with progress in agriculture, knew the need for outlets where the main machinery producers could exhibit their products. True, there were small local agricultural shows, but the need was for something more far-reaching. To this end, the Royal Agricultural Society was formed in 1839. The first show was at Oxford, but the minutes of the Society recall that it was the intention to move the venue each year so that all parts of the country would benefit. Now, not only all interested parties had a chance to see the form progress was taking, but the makers were encouraged by cash prizes to improve and expand their products. The importance that the trade attached to these shows was evident from the start, when Ransome's sent over 5 tons of exhibits to Oxford, despite the fact that it entailed a journey of over one hundred miles by horses and wagons. Now the farmer was able to see the portable engine working as their designers intended. Soon new names began to enter the show ring. Cambridge exhibited one that was possibly the first concept of the modern portable.

Until 1847, the designers had favoured a vertical cylinder. Now they were moving towards the horizontal. With other improvements in the mechanical design, this portable earned the builder a prize of £50 for the best engine on show. Its durability was later to be well proven, for similar models are said to have worked through to the end of the century.

Hornsby of Grantham was another name coming to the fore, with portable engines designed for farming operations. An interesting feature of their engine, which won first prize at the York show in 1848, was the fact that its unique round firebox was later adapted by the famous steam wagon manufacturers, Robey.

A Foster Portable connected up for threshing relives a familiar sight in the farm yards of England during the heyday of such engines

In many ways 1848 saw the arrival of the portable in both town and country. In that year the modern design made its first appearance. The builders were Clayton and Shuttleworth, and their engine had a horizontal cylinder driving forward to a bent crankshaft. It was obtainable in three sizes, 4 h.p., 5 h.p., and 6 h.p. Now, it seemed, steam had been successfully harnessed for the agriculturalist, and those who viewed these models must have doubted if further improvement were possible. Man, however, never stands still. The drawback of the portable was the need for horses to move it from job to job. The strain on the animals, especially during the winter months, was enormous and inevitably, many died from over exertion.

Ransome's believed they had provided the answer in 1849, when they exhibited their "Farmer's Engine" at the Royal Show at Leeds. Not only was it transportable under its own power, but for the first time in the era of steam no horse was needed for steerage. Bevel wheels, operated from the driving position, turned the front wheels in the direction required. Experts who witnessed the unveiling and subsequent tests were lavish in their praise. "Here", one said, "is the universal assistant for all farms. It only requires to be known to be appreciated".

Yet, strange to relate, the experts were wrong. It failed to become universally acknowledged. Ransome's second attempt to introduce a "traction engine", as this machine undoubtedly was, met with the same failure as their earlier self propelled design. The reason is hard to find. Without doubt this was truly a "Farmer's Engine", yet the farmers turned their backs on it. Some have advanced a theory that, as the portable had to fight for recognition in a society deeply averse to change, so this modern conception met with similar response among people who now accepted the portable as part of their daily life. True, change can take a long time among countryfolk, but this hardly explains why such a chance was lost.

The portable, however, had now triumphed over all early setbacks. There was scarcely a farm that did not have at least one engine employed on such diverse tasks as driving a threshing drum, saw bench or chaff cutter. In other capacities they served stone quarries and drove water pumps. It is estimated that, at the height of their power, the east of England alone housed over 60,000 engines.

No better description of the main features of the portable can be found than that given by John Bourne in his "Catechism of the Steam Engine", published in 1848. "The portable engines", he said, "as applied to agriculture, are all similar to one another. They consist of a boiler with an internal firebox and horizontal tubes recembling very much a locomotive boiler. On the top of the boiler is a cylinder with the connecting rod attached to the end of the piston as in a locomotive, and it is the connecting rod that turns the crank of a shaft extending across the top of the boiler. It is this shaft to which pulleys are fitted to communicate the motion of the engine by means of belts to any mechanism to be driven."

John Bourne also had some interesting information to impart that showed how the portable gradually improved as manufacturer vied with manufacturer for a share of the market. The figures given were for Clayton and Shuttleworth's engines from 1849 to 1855, a span of six years. In 1849 their 5 h.p. engine took 44 minutes to get up steam, and used coal at the rate of just over 11lbs per horse power hour. Six years later they had so improved design that an 8 h.p. engine took only 34 minutes to steam up from cold, and then used just over 4lbs of coal per horse power hour.

Bourne made no attempt to hide his own enthusiasm for these remarkable engines, describing them as cheap, simple and efficient. Generally, he said, they would cost the farmer in the region of £35 per horse power. However, for this money he had a machine which was "so simple that even an ignorant farm labourer could assume charge with the minumum of instruction". To stress their efficiency, Bourne stated, that connected to a threshing drum, portables could thresh up to forty quarters of wheat in a ten hour working day, using only 3 cwt of coal and some 300 gallons of water.

To most farmers they were the answer to a long felt need. Mechanisation was no longer a dream, but rather a practical proposition. Indeed, such was the favour with which they were met when fully developed, that several manufacturers continued production into the 1950's for both the home market and overseas. Yet they always had that inherent disadvantage that horses were necessary for movement. Although Ransome's had failed with their "Farmer's Engine" on a national scale, there were many farmers who, recognising the drawbacks in the engines they then used, looked for an alternative. The man who initially supplied the answer was a remarkable Rochester farmer, turned engineer, Thomas Aveling, who was to write the next chapter in the "story of steam".

CHAPTER III

The Father of the Traction Engine

Many men were concerned in the evolution of the traction engine. Names such as Burrell, Robey, and John Fowler, all played their part in seeing that the original basic ideas were brought to fruition. But only one man has been accorded the title of "Father of the Traction Engine" - and he was Thomas Aveling.

Born in Cambridgeshire in 1824, his early life did nothing to indicate the brilliance that would later emerge. In fact, in the eyes of many who knew him in boyhood, Aveling was considered slow and dimwitted. This, in actual fact, was a result of his upbringing. His father died shortly after his birth, and when his mother eventually remarried, it was to provide her son with a step-father who ruled him with a rod of iron. In the face of parental discipline, Thomas Aveling retreated into himself, and his true character was only revealed when he escaped from his home ties. Apprenticed to a farmer in Cambridgeshire, he soon showed an innate mechanical ability. Marriage to the neice of his employer was followed by establishment in his own right as a farmer.

Now his ability in the field of engineering truly came to the fore. Agricultural implements, in those far off days, were primitive in the extreme, and breakdowns were a regular occurrence. Thomas Aveling began his engineering career by repairing such appliances for his immediate neighbours. Soon, however, he was carrying things a stage further and adapted them to a more efficient system. From this it was but a short step to establishing his own engineering works at Rochester in 1850.

From the very beginning Aveling was greatly impressed with the possibility of applying mechanical power to the field of agriculture. As early as 1856 he had made some form of steam plough, for which local Kent farmers presented him with three hundred guineas and a piece of plate in recognition of his achievements. Unfortunately, no record or illustration exists today, so we are unable to see what form it actually took.

By then, of course, the portable was becoming established throughout the countryside, and Aveling welcomed the advances that it brought.

Yet, as he recalled, "it is an insult to mechanical science, to see half a dozen horses drag along a steam engine, and the sight of six sailing vessels towing a steamer would certainly not be more ridiculous".

This drawback in the design of the portable was overcome when Aveling converted a Clayton and Shuttleworth portable to self propulsion, by means of a long driving chain between the crank shaft and rear axle. Yet even this did not make the horse redundant. Although self propulsion had arrived, the animal was an essential between the shafts for steerage purposes. It is interesting to recall that this latest advance did not meet with the universal approval of all farmers. For while the number of horses was reduced from the five or six that were needed for towing, the single steerage horse, with no actual heavy work to do, developed a tendency towards laziness that made it useless when put to work pulling loads or implements.

Aveling, however, was not finished. The conversion of the portable was but the first of many ideas that he had, and in 1859 he took out his first traction engine patent. At that time he did not have manufacturing resources capable

Engines such as this 6 h.p. 12 tons Fowler represent the ultimate in the design of the general purpose engine

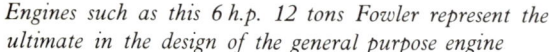

of building traction engines, so he had to approach outside makers to put his ideas into practice, and into this the Lincoln firm of Clayton and Shuttleworth entered with enthusiasm.

The first engine made by the firm to Aveling's design, was exhibited at the Royal Agricultural Society of England's Show at Canterbury in 1860, being advertised as an "8 h.p. Patent Steam Locomotive Engine". In appearance it differed little from that first converted portable, but did away with the annoying requirement of having a horse between the shafts for steering. Yet the shafts themselves were retained, for steering was done by means of a single front wheel mounted in a fork with a bracket attaching it to the shafts.

From the top of the fork a lever extended backwards to be operated by the steersman, who sat with his feet dangling between the shafts. This then, was Aveling's next contribution to the evolution of the traction engine – his "pilot steerage". This primitive form of steerage satisfied Aveling for the next six years or so, and it was only when he concentrated his attention on road roller design that he found its inherent drawback.

A 1915 Burrell General Purpose engine. This machine spent most of its working life in agriculture

By 1861 Aveling was at last in a position to start producing his own engines at Rochester. Soon, at a price of £360, they were finding ready markets in the countryside. Although Thomes Aveling justly deserves his place of honour in the story of the steam traction engine, other makers were working contemporary with him, and adding their ideas to produce what became the ultimate in this form of design.

Self propulsion of the portable by means of chain drive was applied by Garretts, Tuxfords, Clayton and Shuttleworth, Savage, Burrell, and others, until it evolved into a definite class of its own. With the possible exception of Tuxfords who used a vertical enclosed engine, all followed the portable characteristics with cylinders over the firebox, with a crankshaft carrying a large flywheel just behind the chimney. But, as gradual variations were made, these new types of engines began slowly to take on the appearance we recognise today. The first Savage engines had a footplate for the driver, but a separate tender for water. As time passed this was incorporated into the actual engine itself, giving the tank and bunker as an integral part of the design. Aveling's fifth wheel steering, with a man sitting on the front of the engine manoeuvering it into the required direction by means of the "pilot steerage" was obviously not an efficient answer. Hence the design followed by Aveling of the ship's wheel and chain was itself taken over by the long life chain and bobbin steering worked from the traction engine platform.

Methods of applying the final drive varied from maker to maker. Some favoured chain, while others looked to gear drive. Without doubt one of the main faults in these early engines was in their final chain drive, for at that time the only type of chain available was the crude and unpredictable pitch chain. Breakdowns were frequent and there was little the makers could do but turn their attention to gear drive. If the modern roller link chain had then been available, it is possible that traction engine design would have followed a totally different path. However, this was not to be.

Such was the progress made in the design of the General Purpose Traction Engine that, in the comparatively short space of ten years, Thomas Aveling, had progressed from that first primitive engine to a model that included nearly all the features we expect today. Gear drive was now the rule rather than the exception; steering was by chain and bobbin; water tanks were an integral part of the engine, and coal was carried in a bunker behind the driver.

Three requirements had yet to be accomplished: compounding, road springing, and the use of differential gears. The basic design, however, had arrived. Compounding, the method whereby steam from a high pressure cylinder is fed at a lower pressure after having once done its work, into a low pressure cylinder, was perfected by both Fowler and Aveling and introduced in 1881.

A 1911 Clayton and Shuttleworth single cylinder machine used for threshing

Springing was a feature that puzzled designers for many years. The front axles presented no problems, but the position in regard to the drive axle was a different matter. Fowlers tackled the problem from the aspect of springing the wheels themselves, using a system whereby the weight of the engine was supported by sprung spokes, with an arm projecting from the hub and connected, via springs, to the rim to absorb driving stresses. Others, such as Burrell, tackled springing of the drive axle direct.

The difficulty was that this had to be arranged in such a way that the up and down movement did not affect the meshing of the gear teeth. By an elaborate system the firm arranged that the axle and the main drive end of a countershaft were free to move in an upwards or downwards position without affecting the mesh of the gears in use. This system was costly and, for a machine designed mainly for agricultural work, unnecessary.

The same can be said of the use of differential gears, whereby one rear wheel can move at a different speed to the other when cornering or taking other such manoeuvres. Again in agriculture where speed was not an absolutely essential requirement, the effect could be obtained by removing the driving pin from one of the rear wheels on acute corners, hence allowing the machine to "freewheel" on one side.

So the General Purpose Traction Engine had arrived in the form we recognise today. From the beginning it was a welcome servant of agriculture, for the traction engine has always belonged more to the countryside than the town. Most makers were, in fact, either agricultural engineers in one form or another, or had been farmers. Aveling we have already discussed. Charles Burrell; Garrett; Clayton and Shuttleworth; Ransomes; Wallis and Stevens, and of course, Taskers, had all started as agricultural engineers. These were the famous names in the traction engine world, but, as always, the demand for engines brought in the smaller makers, anxious to cash in on this new market. Some made few machines, but made them well. Others also made few and made them badly, as is shown by a report in the magazine "Engineer" for 1861, covering the exhibits at the Royal Show.

"One engine, built by someone from Newton le Willows and of only two or three horse power, stood in one corner of the showground, roped off by the committee, who viewed it with distaste. It had but one stay bolt in the

Threshing with a Ransome, Sims and Jefferies General Purpose engine, built in 1914

middle of each side of the firebox, and no stays of any sort in the crown plate. Human safety forbids its makers the chance of a demonstration." Fortunately such manufacturers were rare and one of the most exciting aspects of the age is the engineering excellence that was the rule rather than the exception. Indeed, such was the perfection of the craftsmen who built these engines, that Charles Burrell used to proudly claim that, with every part made by hand, no two of his machines could ever be exactly alike.

The General Purpose Traction Engine was the tool of the countryside, and its most vital task, was at harvest time, when it came into its own driving the great threshing drums. In fact, the threshing drum was in integral part of the equipment of the General Purpose engine and the reason is not hard to find. The actual threshing drum or "box" as it was known to the men who had the unpleasant task of working with it, had predated the traction engine by some ten years or so, and it was indeed a welcome arrival. In the days prior to its introduction, the harvest was threshed by men using a flail - two rounded

Steam as it used to be. A General Purpose engine harnessed up to a threshing drum

*Foster 6 h.p. single cylinder traction engine No. 14593,
built in 1927 and used for general farming duties*

pieces of wood connected by a leather thong, lifted above the head and
brought crashing down on the corn laid out on the hard surface below. The
time taken to thresh even a small harvest was considerable and the introduction of the "box" cut this down drastically.

In appearance the threshing drum is an unwieldy contraption. Made
almost completely of wood, it was fitted with beater bars and adjusted so that
the corn to be threshed was dealt with by a rubbing action, thus separating
the grain from the rest of the ear. The straw itself was passed through the
shakers to make sure no grain remained in it and then either went to a straw
tier to be tied into bundles of about 56 lbs in weight, or a high pressure baler
which made bundles of some one hundredweight or more. The grain itself
was taken to the bottom of the drum where it passed onto a continuous belt,
being carried through a smutter and rotary screen to the top and then
deposited in corn sacks. In the mid-19th century, the 54" drum was in
common use, and in a working day of ten hours could thresh anything up to
eighty hundredweight of corn. Given even the best yield, this meant that one
hundred acres could be finished in about twenty-six days.

For the small farmer it was obviously an uneconomical proposition, for his

1922 Ruston and Hornsby General Purpose engine, used for threshing

drum would be standing idle for the greater part of the year. Even on larger farms the threshing tackle was in use for only a limited period. Although it was possible to drive a threshing drum by horse power, with the animals operating a turntable and the circular motion being transmitted by shaft to the drum, the common form of motive power soon became the portable engine.

Hence the threshing contractor came on the scene, particularly so with the arrival of the General Purpose engine. Although these could act as "maids of all work" about the farm, many farmers liked to hire the services of the outside contractor rather than lay out money to buy a traction engine and the associated threshing drum. It was, in fact, the threshing contractors who made up the bulk of the home market for traction engines.

A typical threshing outfit would usually consist of the traction engine, a 54" drum, a trusser, an elevator for getting the straw bales to the top of the stack, and sometimes a chaff cutter. The latter was used when the farmer asked for the straw to be cut up into feed for his horses. Although the nutritional value was low, the straw gave the animals a well fed feeling.

Although the compound engine had appeared on the scene by 1881, it was the single engine which ruled in the field of the threshing contractor. The general opinion among the men that had to use them, was that the single was better for this particular task. Not only were compounds more expensive in the first place, they were also more difficult to govern at low pressures. Whereas a single would work all day at a pressure of about 80 lbs, the compound needed at least 140 lbs pressure, and this meant more time in first getting up steam with either the driver having to arrive earlier or the whole gang kept waiting. In addition there were far more oiling points on the compound that needed attention during the day's work.

The arrival of the threshing set on any farm was a time of high excitement for the children. Indeed, there are many adults today who, when they talk of the old time threshing tackle feel the blood run fast in their veins.

The men were always under the charge of a foreman, and it was either he or the farmer who decided with which stack to commence work. The drum would be drawn to it, and levelled. This was an essential operation and was carried out with jacks fitted to the drum. The shutters were then let down to make a feeding platform and the elevator placed in position. Meanwhile the driver would slowly bring his engine into position, check it was level with the driving pulleys of the drum, and the belts would be connected up. First the main belt from the drum to engine, and if this was slack the engine had to be backed slightly to get the right tension.Woe betide the crew too idle to remove the belt first. For if the engine reversed too far, the result, at the best, was a twisted shaft·on the main drum which would stop work until repairs had been effected.

Then, when the main belt was in position, the driver would test it in operation with a few turns of the flywheel. In the meantime the farmer's own men had taken the thatch off the top of the stack, removed any damp sheaves and were standing ready for work. The engine would now be set in motion, slowly at first and then building up to the governed speed. When the foreman was satisfied everything was running as it should, the first sheaves would be tossed to the cutter standing on the top of the drum. A deft flick with his knife, the binder twine fell away and the corn was passed to the feeder who spread it out on the drum's belt. Soon the drum settled down to give a steady hum as the beaters began to operate on the ears, and dust would begin to emerge from every crack in the thresher.

To begin with the work was relatively easy. The pitchers on the stack were dropping down to the cutter. The dust was light. But, as the day wore on and the stacks diminished in size, the pitchers were throwing upwards to the men on the drum, and the dust had increased until it clouded the whole scene, finding its way into everything, and adding to the general discomfort. Dust, however, bad as it was, was not the only problem. Rats and mice were serious disturbers of the peace. For, as the lower sheaves were reached, the rodents, secure up to then in their shelter, made a bolt for freedom. Usually farm workers assembled with dogs and sticks and then the fun began. Many mice and indeed rats, on being confronted by such an enemy force, headed for what appeared to be the nearest place of refuge – up the trouser leg of any unfortunate who happened to be standing close by. Hard luck on the man stupid enough to omit to tie binder twine tightly round the trouser legs to foil that avenue of rodent escape.

Threshing in general was not a time enjoyed by the men taking part, and there was often a sigh of relief as the last sheaf was fed into the drum, the dust finally settled and the contracting crew prepared to move to their next job. To the farmer, without any doubt, contractors were a boon, for even as late as 1913 the work was done for a mere £3 per hour, with the hirer supplying coal and water for the traction engine. This, particularly to the farmer in a small way of business, was a vast saving on the hundreds of pounds he would have laid out to buy his own equipment.

Contractors grew during the age of steam and during that time they

1927 Foster, No. 14593. A popular entrant at Midland Rallies

undoubtedly prospered. In Lincolnshire alone, in the year 1896, according to Kelly's directory for the County, no less than two hundred and eighteen agricultural contractors were offering their equipment for hire. As well as the threshing contractor, there were steam plough contractors and cultivator contractors, as well as men hiring out traction engines on their own. Some of course, were vast concerns whose tackle worked a wide area, while others were individual owners anxious to capitalise on their outlay by working for friends and neighbours, more often than not with themselves as engine crew.

It was a tragedy of the steam age that so many who had the foresight to invest in tackle and set up as contractors, were too short sighted to see the end of the era, even when bankruptcy stared them in the face. Many met financial ruin.

Although designed primarily for threshing work, the General Purpose Traction Engine had qualities that made it indispensible in other fields. Nowhere was this more true than in forestry. Trees that had been felled had to be hauled to nearby clear flat ground to be loaded onto carts for transport to the saw mills. A task which, prior to the introduction of the self propelled engine, taxed even the most powerful of horses. To these mechanical horses, of course, it was all in a day's work. Chains would be connected to the tree and the engine exerted its massive force on loads which could weigh anything up to ten tons or more, hauling them away from the cutting area.

Although the traction engine proved suitable for this type of work, it proved hard and difficult for the crews concerned. In winter, when the ground was wet, the wheels would slip and slither as the old steamer sought vainly to find a grip. Then paddles had to be fitted, the engine moved to the firmest piece of ground available, chains run out, and towing started. However, it was not only in the haulage of felled timber that these old engines proved their worth. Often, when instructions were given for an area to be cleared of trees, the condition was included that all roots and stumps also be removed. Here the general purpose engine truly proved its worth and many spent a lifetime in such work. In fact so popular did they become in forestry work, that Fowlers made an engine with a specially designed winding drum for use when stump pulling.

Although the advent of steam freed horses from what had been a killing job, it did little to speed up the process. Working in conditions that would often see a tree felled in thick undergrowth and requiring haulage over a considerable distance to the loading point, speed was something which had to be forgotten. Once the cable had been connected from tree to engine, work could start. Often however, direct haulage failed to move the timber and then the hard work began. Ropes would be fitted round the tree, the engine's cable connected up, and the engine exert its pull while remaining stationary. Then, if the terrain was really bad the whole procedure would be gone through again with gradual fifty yard pulls eventually getting the offending tree either to hard ground where direct traction could be used, or to where the cart was waiting to take the timber to the saw mill.

Even at the saw mill the traction engine proved its true ability, for many worked continuously in the mill, providing the power for the saw benches. Indeed, from the early days of the self propelled engine, many makers offered saw benches in various sizes as equipment to be bought with the engine.

This was, of course, a logical extension of their use. During the early days of steam, forestry was, in the main, confined to large estates. Timber felled in the woods and forest would be brought to their own saw mills, where it was cut up for use as fencing posts and for repair work on buildings and barns. Hence an engine required for threshing during the harvest time could be later be used by woodmen for haulage at the site, or kept in the mill to power the saw benches as the timber was cut up into various sizes.

There were also outside owners in the timber clearance and haulage business, who bought and used traction engines for contract work in the field of wood felling and haulage, working wherever there was a need for their services. The work of such owners increased rapidly with the outbreak of the Great War.

Before then, timber had found its main use in the countryside, but it was suddenly in demand, both for pit props to meet the ever increasing need for coal, and as reinforcement for trenches the troops prepared on the Western Front.

Soon timber contractors were working every hour possible supplying the needs of the nation. And as the need for timber increased so, of course, did the demand for traction engines for work which was now accepted as being virtually impossible without them.

So when it is considered that these engines could carry out every function that the portable had been found capable of, as well as forestry work and hauling produce about the farm and to market, they truly deserved their title "Jack of All Trades".

Even today the design knowledge and engineering experience that these old engines gave to their designers is remembered through the ability of Fosters of Lincoln. This firm, always renowned for their truly splendid engines during the period up to 1914, turned their knowledge to building the first British military tank in 1915. It was an achievement that they allowed no one to forget, and every engine that left the Lincoln works after that date, carried an emblem of this new form of military vehicle. It is interesting, on the rally field today, to seek out the Foster engines and look for that primitively designed tank that is proudly worn on the bottom of the smoke box door and recall that this period of engineering excellence saw also the birth of what has become a complex fighting machine.

One final point regarding these old General Purpose engines is their classification by n.p.h. – nominal horse power – rather than as we now use, the general h.p. rating. It is said that the whole intention of this early system was to confuse. While today it might confuse the uninitiated, we were not intended to be the victims of the deception.

This nominal horse power rating is, in fact, only about one seventh of the actual horse power, and was a device brought into being when steam manufacturers and engine owners were fighting the diehard attitudes of local authorities and the landed gentry. To describe their engines with but a fraction of their actual power was to make the machine sound less formidable, particularly when consideration was being given to the damage a heavy engine could cause to the primitive road surfaces of that age. Hence, n.h.p. was born of necessity and, once in common use by all makers, it remained the standard by which traction engines were graded.

The general purpose engine was an undoubted success in every field of agriculture, but while it showed its prowess on farm, field and in woodland, it was still the subject of oppressive legislation when it left private land for the public roads.

CHAPTER IV

The Arrival of Road Haulage

"If I send a boiler weighing 15 tons and drawn by 15 horses over a bridge, and that bridge breaks, I have nothing to pay. However, if I send that same load drawn by a traction engine over the same bridge, and it then breaks, I am fully responsible for the damage."

Those words by Thomas Aveling adequately summed up the position of traction engines on the road. Whereas a team of horses engaged in normal day to day haulage could, at that time, tear up the surface and leave it a mass of ridges and hollows, without a word of complaint, even the slightest damage caused by a steam engine would make the owner and driver liable to legal action.

The 1831 "Red Flag Act" is these days looked upon as a joke, but to the owners of those steam traction engines it was only one item of repressive legislation which they had to endure. Because of it, no traction engine was allowed on a public highway unless it was preceded by a man walking 60 yards ahead carrying a red flag, as a warning to other road users of the possible dangers of mechanically propelled transport. Therefore, every engine was restricted to travelling at the same speed as the flag carrier.

Nor was this all. Toll bridge owners had the full protection of the law when it came to allowing these "new fangled belching, smoking monsters" to cross. Often a driver found the cost of passing through these man-made obstructions would amount to as much as 4/- for each ton carried, while a horse drawn load would escape by paying a mere 3d or so per ton.

Local byelaws added to the confusion and hardship that traction engine owners, concerned with road transport, had to endure. In some areas all movement of these engines was forbidden during the hours of daylight, and they were allowed on public roads only after dark, when hardly any other traffic would be expected. There was little the unfortunate owners and drivers could do about the position, and if they appeared before the courts, leniency was unknown. On one occasion, in a vain attempt to prevent the use of a section of road by traction engines, a Turnpike Trust put boulders across the

A Road Haulage engine of 1913

surface. The result was a broken axle for the steamer, which led to a boiler explosion. The cause of the accident was ignored by the authorities, but the engine owner appeared before the court and was fined for it and the resultant damage.

Relief, in a small way, came with the passing of the Locomotive Act of 1878. Contrary to popular belief, it was this Act and not the one of 1896 that did away with the need for the infamous red flag, although it still required a man to walk in front of the engine at the reduced distance of 20 yards. As a further concession the machines were allowed to travel at 4 m.p.h. in open country and at 2 m.p.h. when passing through a town or village.

Repression, however, was still the order of the day. Every Local Authority was given the power to prohibit the use of steamers on roads in their area for any eight hours during a period of twenty four. This meant, in many cases, that the man concerned with road haulage by steam was forced to travel at least part of the way, during the hours of darkness. In those days of primitive lighting and roads, accidents were inevitable. In fact, more than one expert has put the blame for many fatalities arising from traction engine accidents, on the doorstep of those who saw fit to authorise such laws.

Another blow to those who saw a future for steam haulage was the decision, in the 1878 Act, to authorise Local Authorities to levy a £10 licence fee from every traction engine owner who used their roads. This was particularly hard on the man whose engines crossed into many different areas, for the licence fee was levied by each.

The penalty for not conforming was a £2 fine and although some owners, going into a particular area infrequently, chose to ignore the demand for the licence, the police were ever vigilant. Many found, to their cost, that the amount paid in fines came to more than the £10 levy. Some ignored it on principle but, in the main, it was one more piece of oppression that the road haulier had to live with. Partial relief came in 1896 when the Locomotives on Highways Act received royal approval.

Providing the unladen weight did not exceed three tons and pulled only one trailer, the restriction of having a man walk in front was removed, as was the provision that each machine must carry a steersman as well as an engine man. The new specifications attracted some new manufacturers, who provided mainly single cylinder machines, although some compounds found their way onto the market.

Tractors did not figure greatly in the story of steam until 1903, when the Motor Car Act of that year divided road locomotives into two distinct classes; heavy locomotives and light locomotives. The former, weighing over five tons, still required two crew members and their speeds were held at two miles per hour in built-up areas, and four miles per hour in open country. Engines weighing under five tons, however, could be operated by one man and travel at a maximum speed of 5 m.p.h. This was a signal for many more builders to turn their attentions to lighter engines. Such units became invaluable for light haulage, and were fashionable with furniture removers, timber hauliers and travelling showmen.

The most famous tractor of all was, without a doubt, a Tasker's 4 n.h.p. "Little Giant" single cylinder engine, which quickly gained the title "The Horses Friend". At that time horses, used for road haulage, were subjected to the hardest of work. They were expected to drag heavy carts up the steepest inclines, with their owner more concerned with the financial viability of his business than the conditions under which his horses worked.

Nowhere was this more true than at the steep Anerley Hill, near Crystal Palace in London. Daily, people living nearby, witnessed the spectacle of horses almost dropping with fatigue, hauling their loads to the top of the hill, urged on by whip and voice. The sight so enraged two sisters living nearby that in 1903 they purchased a "Little Giant" from Taskers, and instructed the driver they engaged to position the engine at the foot of the hill and use it

A Fowler Road haulage engine, typical of the machines that
hauled heavy loads to every part of the country

whenever he saw a horse, obviously overloaded, or in a poor state of health, approaching. It was said that it became so familiar a sight that horses grew accustomed to it and refused the upward pull whenever it was positioned for work. An interesting aside to the story is that after working at the job for many years the engine was eventually returned to the makers for preservation, and in 1969 sold for the grand sum of £4,000.

Tractors proved to be of great value to Local Authorities. With this reliable and hardy form of steam power, they had the facilities for hauling road making material, drawing the trailers concerned with clearing soil, and the hundred and one transportation jobs that arose in every town and city. Now those very people who had imposed oppressive legislation on road hauliers were themselves turning to this form of power for their needs. The change in attitude is not difficult to understand.

In 1870 the bicycle arrived on the scene, and it opened up road travel to a new section of the community - the middle classes. Priced in the region of £10, cycles were obviously out of the reach of the working man, and at such a price and with the requirement of physical effort for their propulsion, they held no attraction for the aristocracy. Hence, the school teachers, shop keepers and merchants of the age were the people who began the cycling craze that hit England. And it did indeed become a craze. From 1896 when the first periodical devoted to the sport, "Bicycling News", was introduced, until 1898, no less than twenty such publications came on sale in England.

With the introduction of the cycle and its rapid popularity came a cry for better roads. It was a cry that could not be ignored. The formation of the various County Councils in 1888 was a step in the right direction, and soon active consideration was being given to improving the lot of this new travelling public. However, road building required a form of transport more reliable and more powerful than the horse. It already existed on the farm, now it was the time for its use in towns.

Old prejudices were therefore partly forgotten and, although steam was not welcomed with open arms, it was accepted as a necessary form of road vehicle, and the various Acts of Parliament laid the foundations for road haulage to develop.

In its final form, the Light Steam Tractor was a versatile and useful steam engine. With the advent of the 5 ton weight limit, the designs increased until compounds outnumbered single cylinder engines. Most carried up to fifty yards of steel rope on a winch fitted to the back axle. This was invaluable for hauling loads standing on soft ground which would not give traction to the engine itself. With the engine on hard ground and the rear wheels scotched to prevent them slipping, the load could be hauled across, and away went the engine. The smaller engines thought nothing of hauling a load weighing seven tons for nearly ten miles while burning only one hundredweight of coal. As they could travel some thirty miles without stopping for water, they were a good investment for anyone with an interest in the field of light haulage.

As interesting as these tractors are, it is the heavyweights that really established the haulage industry. In the beginning it was the general purpose engines that were brought into the field of heavy haulage, but gradually the designs were changed and road locomotives fell into a class of their own. These massive engines were almost always of compound design, with a canopy to protect the crew from the worst of the elements, a belly tank to carry extra water, and solid rubber tyres on all wheels. Sprung axles had become common by the end of the 1880's, and soon three-speed gearing was a further standard feature.

The very first engine ever built specially for use on roads for haulage purposes came from the Thetford works of Charles Burrell in 1856; a fact that is today commemorated by a plaque on the wall of what used to be the drawing offices of this famous firm. Nearly every steam manufacturer tried his hand at road locomotives at one time or another, but without doubt the most popular among the large haulage firms were the products from Burrell, Fowler, Foster and McLaren.

The excellence of the engineering standards of those days is clearly shown by the three 12 n.p.h. McLaren locomotives which were acquired in 1886 by the French government for Post Office use. Every year these engines covered a total of 15,000 miles over roads that barely merited the use of that name, maintaining an average of seven to eight miles per hour over the seventy mile journey from Lyons to Grenoble, their daily beat.

Fowler "Big Lion" and "Super Lion" were other engines that found favour with the larger haulage contractors. Without doubt, in the field of heavy haulage, power was a prime necessity, for road transport came into its own for tasks with which the railways could not cope.

Large machinery, boilers and other appliances that were impossible to move by rail could be slowly but surely taken across the length and breadth of the country by these massive road locomotives. Often more than one engine was used. A good example of this was seen as late as 1938, when three "Super Lions" transported what has been said to be the world's largest indivisible load, a steam accumulator 70' long and 12' in diameter, from the engineering works of Cochrane's in Annan, Scotland, to Beckton Gas Works in London.

The journey, which began on the 6th January, took eighteen working days to complete, with speeds averaging 2 m.p.h. The only trouble was reported when the load was travelling over Shap, where snow made traction difficult. Two engines performed the actual haulage work with the third travelling as a reserve and drawing the living van in which the crews slept.

Another notable journey was made by the appropriately named, and now famous, Super Lion "Atlas". This also involved the moving of an accumulator from Annan to Glasgow. Although the distance was not comparable with that undertaken later by its brothers, "Atlas" had the distinction of pulling the 120 ton load unaided. Although speed was, of necessity, slow, such epics proved beyond doubt the ability and reliability of these great haulage engines.

The journey, however, was not all. No long distance haulage could be considered until the whole route had been checked and tested and each bridge authority given at least two days notice of the intention to transport the load. In fact, it is said that the 1938 journey was planned for a full eighteen months before it actually commenced. When it is considered that sometimes bridges had to be specially strengthened to allow the passage of such weights, the time period is understandable.

When road haulage was accepted by local authorities, many went out of their way to assist the haulage firms, going as far, in one case, as lowering a road under a bridge in order that road locomotives and their great loads could be accommodated.

The work for the crews was long, arduous and dangerous. They thought

1927 Wallis and Stevens oil bath tractor which came into being when the story of steam on the road was in decline

nothing of cutting away country hedgerows and banks to allow the load to pass, or sawing off overhanging branches in order that an exceptionally high piece of equipment could safely be driven under them. Their ingenuity became legend. To get a load round a right angle corner that was too narrow for it, they would run the wheels onto steel plates and then push or pull the trailer round, with the aid of the road locomotive or another if they happened to be travelling in convoy. Incidents have been recorded where the lighting of a whole street has been dismantled to let some particularly wide load through, and tram wires and other overhead obstructions were taken down on innumerable occasions.

The firms that pioneered this heavy transport business in England became almost household words throughout the country: Kerrs of Glasgow; Edward Box of Liverpool; Norman E. Box of Manchester; and Coupe Bros. of Sheffield. Pickfords, still known today, bought out Norman Box and Coupe Bros., and incorporated their road locomotives into their own fleet.

Their loads included every form of heavy material. The handsome bronze statue of King Alfred at Winchester stands on a 40 ton granite pedestal, but both, together with the supporting 25 ton granite base, were hauled from the quarry in Cornwall by two great Fowler engines.

An interesting point about this particular journey is that one engine was pulling the load and the other following to provide braking power. When travelling downhill, the rear machine would then take the weight of the load and so hold it back to prevent it overrunning or forcing itself onto the front engine. The second engine, of course, could be brought into use on steep upward gradients, reducing the strain on the towing engine. With really heavy loads three engines would be used.

One can today only imagine the scene as these great steamers progressed slowly but surely through the streets of our towns and cities; truly such power had never been seen before and, in an age of compactness, will never be seen again. Steam was not confined to the usual. On one occasion a road locomotive was called upon to help at the launching of a Blackburn flying boat in 1928. Only steam could provide the power required to haul the great aeroplane from its slipway to the launching point. For normal haulage, steel shod bogies were used and although these proved admirable for the job in hand, they did tend to tear up road surfaces, and, of course, the haulier was responsible for subsequent repairs.

Fowlers came up with a modification in 1927 when they designed a trailer fitted with sixteen wheels each with rubber tyres. Originally designed to transport large pieces of electrical equipment, it soon found favour in nearly every field of heavy haulage and, in fact, when the internal combustion engine took over, a similar trailer was used, to be developed through to the heavy load carriers that we see on our roads today.

The steam trailer was designed to carry a load approaching ninety tons in weight. And, with a knowledge of the obstacles to be overcome, was so made that its actual height from the ground was no more than 2 feet. There were four bogies, each with four wheels; two steerable ones fitted at the front, with the remaining two side by side at the rear. Each bogey could tilt fore and aft and the wheels themselves were made to tilt sideways when the pressure of the load so demanded. In addition, all the back wheels were braked. It was, without doubt, a truly remarkable piece of engineering. And when one considers that it was built from solid steel and had nearly 5,000 rivets to ensure its strength, the asking price of £3,000 was not, perhaps, as expensive as it at first seems.

Another legal concession was made in 1923 when the weight limit for a light locomotive was raised to $7\frac{1}{4}$ tons, but by this time the internal combustion engine had arrived on the scene and sadly steam, as a factor in heavy haulage, was already on the way out. Some firms such as Garrett did in fact construct to this new weight, but their tractors were due for a short life. Even the law of 1926, which decreed that all traction engines for road use be fitted with solid rubber tyres, did nothing to prolong their life. These tyres gave extra resilience to the running of the engines and increased their speed, but once again steam was lagging behind the internal combustion engine. The latter had already reached the stage of pneumatic tyres, and soon motor lorries began to replace the light locomotive at an alarming pace.

The heavy locomotives lasted longer than their smaller brothers, some hauling loads of up to ninety tons well into the 1950's. These, however, were the exceptions to the rule. In general, the internal combustion engine was pushed from all quarters at the expense of the steamers. In 1930 and 1934 legislation added to the taxes for running steam vehicles, and they were taken off the road in their thousands. The costs were now prohibitive and many fleet owners faced ruin when the finality of the situation was forced upon them.

CHAPTER V

Showground Locomotives

Generally speaking, traction engines were utility machines, designed for a particular purpose. Be it threshing, general farm duties, cultivation or the haulage of heavy loads, these grand old machines were made with that task in mind. In the age of perfection in engineering, there was no place for the purely decorative; everything had to be functional.

There are, however, exceptions to every rule and this applied also in the days of steam. One class of user gave to their machines a personality equal to their own. They were, of course, the travelling showmen. Today the engines that formerly lived and worked on the fairgrounds of England are the centre of attraction at every meeting they attend.

The reason is not hard to understand. Here is the absolute perfection that came with the age of steam, not only in mechanical design, but also in the very appearance that gave these old fairground giants an aura of mystery even in their own times. Gleaming brass stanchions support a full length canopy; electric light bulbs hang from the same canopy to give a kaleidoscope of colour and brilliance as the sun sets on the scene. If this is not enough to command admiration, each engine is beautifully painted, as if vying with their rivals to display, in colourful yet tasteful brilliance, the artistic merit of their owners.

Yet this is not all, for almost every Showman's locomotive has a name of it's own. How those names rolled off the tongue in the days when people flocked to the fairgrounds. There would be the "Iron Maiden" proudly proclaiming to the world at large that both she and her owner were "Mighty in Strength and Endurance". Who would argue with that sentiment. "General Buller", that great Brown and May engine; "Earl Haigh"; "The Baillie"; "Dreadnought"; "Queen Mary"; these and many others thrilled the crowds wherever they appeared.

Today the survivors have a following of their own; people who visit the various Rallies and meetings to pay homage to the beauty, magnificence, and above all the usefulness that was and still is to be found on the Showman's

Road Locomotive. For, although their external appearance gives them a charm that is all their own, beauty in this case is but skin deep. Beneath the paint and brass work was an ability to serve their masters as no other form of mechanisation could.

The travelling showmen needed a reliable form of motive power. Before the introduction of the steam traction engine, they had to rely on horses moving their rides and amusements from site to site. Not only was this slow, but also costly: the animals had to be bought and fed, and men employed to look after them. In many cases these men were interested only in the welfare of their charges, and when the fair was pitched they did little general work, leading a life of semi-retirement once they had attended to the animals. They also had to be kept on when the fair was in winter quarters, which all added to the overall cost.

The honour of being the first showman to use a traction engine belongs to an American circus owner, Jim Myers. On Saturday 13th August 1859, Folkestone thrilled to the sight of the circus carriages, then on tour in

A Showman's Road Locomotive, the "Baillie", a 1911 Burrell used on Lancashire fairgrounds until 1945

England, being pulled through the streets in grand procession by a Bray self propelled traction engine. This however, was an isolated incident, brought about more by the novelty of the engine rather than its practical use as a haulage vehicle. In fact, the very use of the engine attracted crowds who would otherwise have had little interest in the circus itself. It was not until the 1880's that traction engines began to find general favour among these travelling fairground people. In the first place, of course, they used the same general purpose engines as the farmer and other road users.

Things were soon to change, for one of the great wonders of the 1880's was the introduction of electric lighting. The dazzling and brilliant light which could be obtained by transmitting a powerful electric current between two sticks of carbon was first shown to the Royal Institute by Sir Humphrey Davy in 1813. This, of necessity had to employ a battery containing no less than 2,000 cells. Another drawback was the fact that as the carbon rods got smaller during their gradual consumption, there was no way of keeping the

Burrell 6 h.p. Compound Showman's engine, No. 3979.
This example, "Earl Haig", was made in 1924

gap between them constant. However, by the early 1850's regulators were developed that solved this problem.

Electric lighting had arrived, but for the showman, to whom it could provide a much needed form of lighting and power, the insurmountable obstacle was the massive batteries required. The show people watched with envy as this new form of light appeared in halls and houses. Then came the breakthough that they had been waiting for. With Faraday's discovery of magnetic electric induction, the dynamo and generator became a practical proposition.

The first generating plant capable of being mounted on a traction engine was the work of R. E. B. Crompton who, in 1879, designed just such equipment for Marshalls of Gainsborough. In July of that year, it is recorded, one of these Marshall-Crompton engines was used to illuminate the Henley Regatta. As can be imagined, the event drew crowds in their thousands, and not all came merely to see and marvel. Many, failing to understand these latest scientific advances and fearful for the future, made determined attempts

A 1911 Brown and May Showman's engine, "General Buller"

"Earl Haig", the 1924 Burrell with companion engine, a 1913 Burrell Showman's

to sabotage the engine and generators. Fortunately, Marshalls had been prepared for this eventuality, and men from Gainsborough, armed with heavy spanners, successfully fought off the intending saboteurs.

In 1886, Thomas Aveling produced his first traction engine designed with the Showman in mind. This was one of his standard cylinder engines with a platform erected over the front of the horn plates, i.e. over the actual motions of the engine, on which a generator was mounted, being driven by a gear ring mounted to the inside of the flywheel. To the fair people, such engines were the answer to their prayers. Now they had a machine that could not only haul their rides and amusements between sites, but on arrival provide the power to drive those self same rides.

Electricity began to provide the power for all fairground requirements. It must be realised, however, that in those early days, lighting was still in the form of arc lamps, the carbon rods of which sparked behind a reinforced glass globe, provided to prevent injury in the event of shattering, which was a fairly common occurrence.

Aveling's original design was soon followed by an engine that carried the generator on a platform at the front of the smoke box, in the position that we recognise today.

John Fowler was another who, in the same year that Aveling decided to enter the field, brought out an engine modified to showman's needs. This again was an engine from their normal range – a compound general purpose with a generator platform fixed by angle iron to the front of the smoke box.

Gradually designs changed until, in 1893, Fowler's were producing a Showman's engine with the generator platform an integral part of the design. Surprisingly enough, the full length canopy, today a feature of every engine of this type, was neglected for some considerable time. It would seem that no consideration was given to the protection of either the crew or the working parts.

By the end of the 19th century the canopy made an appearance. Possibly popular demand among those buying and using the engines forced this on the builder. However, whatever the reason, the Showman's engine had evolved into the class that we have come to love so much. The colourful brass stanchions had also appeared, as supports for the canopy, and a chimney extension was supplied as standard for use when the engine was acting as a stationary generator, so that the smoke could be more easily dispersed. Even the brilliant paintwork and contrasting lining had come to be accepted as standard.

In fact, so perfect had the design of these old steamers become that they continued without the need of modification until the Great War. Then, with an ever increasing public appetite for enjoyment, the amusement caterers turned their attentions to even bigger and more exciting rides, such as the "scenic railways". Although these were an impressive sight with their gaily painted cars and colourful electric lighting they presented a fresh problem both for the showmen themselves and steam engine designers.

Not only had the cars to be manhandled off the rails and on to trailers for travelling, but the load required to start them was beyond the capabilities of most standard generators fitted to Showman's locomotives. Hence Burrell, for one, came up with a special "Scenic Engine". These had a larger boiler than normal, a subsidiary booster dynamo known as an exciter to provide the surge of extra current needed to start the scenics, and a crane for use when loading and unloading.

Here now were veritable power houses in miniature, comprising the locomotive for road haulage, a generating station capable of supplying all necessary power, and a steam crane in its own rights. When beautifully polished, they were indeed a joy to look at. At one stage, Fowler's B.6 engines had even their boilers lagged with aluminium. Surprisingly, although these are among the best loved of all steam traction engines, and the ones most readily called to mind when the age of steam is discussed, the total number built was not great. In fact, between the period 1885 to 1934 the sum total of Showman's locomotives turned out by the various makers was only 411.

Garrett Showman's Tractor, No. 33818, "Wendy", supplied new in 1922

The most prolific manufactures were Burrell, Fowler and Foster, but others also turned their attentions at some time to the needs of the travelling showmen. A breakdown shows the individual outputs as follows:— Charles Burrell of Thetford, 207; John Fowler of Leeds, 82; William Foster of Lincoln, 68; McLaren of Leeds, 16; Wallis and Stevens of Basingstoke, 13; Fodens of Sandbach, 10; Garrett of Leiston, 5; Savage Bros. of Kings Lynn, 5; Aveling and Porter, 2; Ransomes of Ipswich, 2; while Hornsby of Grantham, Lincolnshire, built but one solitary engine to such specifications.

The last engine to carry the proud name of Charles Burrell appeared in 1930 but, ironically, it was actually made by Garretts at their Leiston works. This was due to the fact that Burrells themselves were but one of the many steam builders to face the ignominy of bankruptcy, and all their orders thereafter were completed by Garretts. Despite this, when the engine No. 4092, a three speed, eight horse power model, was collected by its owner, Mrs · Deakin of Brynmawr, it proudly bore the name of that famous Norfolk firm. on the valve chest and wheel hubs.

After many years working in the fairgrounds of Wales, "Simplicity", as the engine was called, was purchased for road haulage work by Kerr's of Glasgow. There, with the dynamo and bracket removed, and canopy cut away at the front, it performed sterling service until, sadly, it ended its life on a scrap heap.

Strangely, the last Fowler Showman's locomotive followed a similar pattern throughout its working life, but with a happier ending. This engine, "Supreme", No. 20223, left the Leeds works in 1934, again bound for that famous showwoman, Mrs. Deakin. And a grand sight it must have been, for Mrs. Deakin had given instructions that this was to be the finest Showman's engine the firm had ever produced, money being no object. Without doubt, "Supreme" was aptly named, and it gained considerable attention wherever it happened to be working. Alas, the day came when it had powered its last ride, and it also found its way to Kerr's of Glasgow. This time, however, when its second working life came to an end, it escaped total destruction, but only just. For some years it was left to rot in a field in Surrey, where it was discovered by a preservationist. After much patient work, "supreme" was eventually restored to its original condition, and today is a welcome visitor to Rally fields in many parts of the country.

Showmen, of course, were intensely proud of their engines, a fact that is borne out by the care and attention lavished on them during their working life, and the way in which the majority, when a new locomotive was required, would spend hours with the builders discussing the paintwork, finish, and any other extras they considered necessary. Small wonder that Charles Burrell once boasted that no two engines from his factory were exactly alike.

For the builders, life was never devoid of interest when dealing with these showground characters. The unexpected became commonplace, and Burrell himself recounted how, on one occasion, when a fairground caterer had finally placed an order for a new engine, he went to his old one, returned with two large bags and emptied them onto the maker's desk. The contents, part of his takings for that season just finished, were left as a deposit on the new engine.

Showman's locomotives were, above all else, long distance travellers. And their drivers saw to it that they were fast runners. A journey of a hundred or so miles would rarely take longer than twelve hours, even when the engines were pulling four laden trailers weighing a total of nearly thirty tons. Even hills with a gradient of one in seven caused them little difficulty, and when a steeper incline was encountered it was a simple matter to uncouple the two rear wagons and let the engine make the pull in two relays.

Showman's engines were fitted with three speeds, slow, intermediate and top. In top, such was the power of these giants of steam that many drivers regularly drove along with a full load at speeds of up to eighteen miles per hour.

Among all Showman's engines, few would dispute the claim that Fowler's were the fastest. Indeed, many owners gladly let their competitors leave the fairground site first, confident in the knowledge that, before the journey's end, their own Fowler would have gaily sailed past the others to make sure of first arrival at the next stopping point.

Although the number of Showman's locomotives built by the various makers was small, others did find their way into fairground life. Sometimes road haulage machines would be bought by showmen and converted by them. On other occasions, such engines would be acquired and taken back to the makers to be adapted to the specifications for their new role.

Steam wagons, to some degree, also figured in fairground life. Foden adapted some of their wagons with a dynamo mounted on an extension in front of the smoke box, and with the canopy extended forward over the dynamo and supported by the familiar brass stanchions. In 1920 the company also produced their "D" type tractor which in many ways resembled their steam wagons, but without the actual wagon part at the rear. Instead, a coal tender was towed. From this, Foden produced a Showman's engine with an overall canopy and generator.

Savages also entered the field, but in their case the generator was mounted to the rear of the driving position, and powered by a separate engine, with the actual wagon part being retained. Another type of engine used in small

1914 Burrell Showman's Engine

quantities on fairgrounds was the centre engine. This was designed to directly power "gallopers" and other such rides. In the beginning these engines were modified portable engines with plates extending upwards from the sides and carrying a roundabout turntable on which the ride could be erected. The smoke and exhaust from the portable went up a flue which led into the hollow vertical shaft at the centre of the "gallopers". Although these did away with much erection work, they were never really popular among the fairground fraternity, being the heaviest part of the load when moving site.

In 1898 Frederick Savage of King's Lynn designed a self moving centre engine. This was, in actual fact, an 8 h.p. single cylinder road machine modified as the portables had been. Although other makers also entered the field, they were never fully accepted by the people who had to use them, and many were finally converted back to their conventional design. In the world of the travelling amusement caterer, the conventional design with its generator, and possibly a crane, could not be bettered and most makers saw a permanent future in this. However, it was not to be.

Although steam lasted longer in active use with these travelling showmen than in other sphers, the end was inevitable. Its coming was hastened by World War II when, in their various theatres of action, the armed forces required not only heavy haulage vehicles, but mobile generators too; the very qualities that steam gave to the travelling showmen. Hence, at the end of the war, as these fairground people began to pick up the threads of their business, the Army was trying to find buyers for equipment now surplus to their needs. Here, for the showman was the chance to purchase, cheaply, both his haulage and generating equipment. So, the glory of the old road locomotives gave way to the comparatively drab but functional diesel engines vehicles, and their equally unimpressive but reliable generators.

So it seemed that another aspect of our life was to disappear forever. And, indeed, if it had not been for that small band of dedicated preservationists, it could so easily have died for all time. However, many of the old Showman's engines found their way into the hands of such enthusiasts, and many showmen themselves, out of a love for the engines that had served them faithfully over so many years, kept them in honourable retirement. Today, through their efforts, we can relive the glory at the steam fair. And not merely through the engines themselves for, more often than not, the steam meeting is graced by the same rides which, in the era of steam, were powered by those great engines.

Of all the fairground rides, of course, the roundabouts are the most familiar. It is interesting to recall that it was in 1865 that steam was first applied to them. In that year S. G. Soames brought his steam driven round-abouts to Aylesham Fair, in Norfolk. This began a progress that was to revolutionise the fairground.

A 1922 Garrett Showman's Tractor, No. 33818

Until this time, roundabouts had been poor, primitive affairs, depending on either man or horse for their power. Speeds were slow and uncertain, and further development seemed impossible. Although Soames could not claim universal success for his conversion, it was his idea that led Frederick Savage, an ironmaster and maker of fairground rides, to further experiments. By 1870 he had perfected steam power for these amusements.

The steam engine was mounted in the centre of the ride, on a sprung truck, and it is this centre truck that made all further development possible. Through gearing, the motion could be carried to the carriages which were suspended from the spinning frame. Be they horses of the old familiar "galloper", or other forms, the means were now available for variations in speed and plane of motion. Without doubt, the work of Savage gave the fairground showmen their finest period. The classic galloping horses, either three or four abreast, soon gave way to other carriages, motor cars or exotic animals. Today the gallopers have lost a lot of their popularity. Possibly, with the advent of new and more daring rides, they appear slow and lacking in thrills, yet, with the growth of the Steam Engine Rallies and Steam Fairs, there has been a fresh surge of enthusiasm for them. "Scenics", although late

A 1922 Burrell Showman's Engine, "Dragon"

"Supreme", the last Fowler to be made

arrivals on the scene, are other old faithfuls that give to the fairground the atmosphere that we came to expect in the age of steam.

All these amusements had a character of their own, as did the great engines that powered and pulled them. Their decoration varied according to the views of their owners, but all were resplendent with gaily coloured carvings, brilliant paintwork, and every other type of adornment that could be tastefully included.

G. T. Tuby's "Gondolas" are a classic example of how the showmen of old transferred their own personality to their amusements. Known throughout the fairground world as "Tuby's Circular Railway", this was a beautiful ride with an abundance of carved work, all painted in gold, with pictures of all the famous Boer War Generals on the droppers. A patriotic touch indeed. Each pillar was resplendent with a carved figure, and the central barrel organ had further revolving figures working from it. The gondolas stayed with the ride until 1906 when, acknowledging the public's love of change, motor cars were used instead and it was given the grand title of "Tuby & Sons 60 h.p. Panhard Motors".

The owner of these gondolas was a man with a very definite personality. As well as being a very active amusement man, he devoted as much of his spare time as possible to civic duties in his home town of Doncaster. In typical showman's style, his progress in local politics was proudly proclaimed by his various Burrell Showman's engines. The first, naturally, was called

Foster 7 h.p. Compound Showman's engine,
No. 14153 "Admiral Beatty", built in 1916

"Councillor' to celebrate his election to the council. As he rose to higher office so Burrell's "Alderman" and "Mayor" set out from Doncaster at the start of each fairground season, to remind the public that here was one showman who had the interests of others truly at heart. A touch of sadness must have accompanied the purchase of that other famous Burrell of G. T. Tuby's, "Ex-Mayor", but throughout its working life this particular engine stood as a memorial to the good work done by this remarkable showman.

Although, to the uninitiated, fairground rides may have appeared more or less identical to their neighbours, to their owners and the more knowledgeable among fairground visitors, these old rides had a personality of their own.

There would be Pat Collins' Loop the Loop Motor Cars, made by Savages and fitted with an 89 key Marenghi in the centre. It was a regular visitor to all the fairs in the Midland Counties of England. William Wilson's Rodeo Swithchback shows how some of the rides evolved. This started life in the ownership of another famous showman, James Pettigrove, as a Chariot Switchback. However, as it passed into the possession of Mr. Wilson, he adapted the track and central truck to fit his own ideas. Originally motor cars formed the ride itself, but later these were superseded by animal figures such as Teddy Bears, Rupert the Cat etc. Even the organs were changed over the years until, in the early 1920's it was fitted with a magnificent Marenghi, with the smaller Gavi made into a unique type of pay box and placed at the side of the ride. With such originality and care, it is small wonder that many sets of amusements that first saw life in the late 1890's are still giving yeoman service to this day.

Other thrills that awaited the visitor to the fairground in those days included Harry Lee's famous steam yachts, yet another ride to have survived to modern times, and a most popular attender at many Rallies and meetings held in various parts of the country. In fact, so popular is this particular reminder of steam fairs of old, that organisers vie with each other in order to ensure its presence at their own meeting.

These steam yachts, or steam swings as they could be more accurately described, consist of two heavy swing "boats" each carrying a number of passengers. They are powered by a stationary engine situated between the two boats, which through a series of chains and gears produces the swinging action. Today only two sets surive: Harry Lee's and Lings', and both have a place of honour in any story devoted to the age of steam for, along with the various other rides, they provided the general public with more pleasure than they could get from most other means.

Today, of course, fairground rides have developed out of all recognition with the ones that were so familiar. Yet these modern rides have not broken the grip of the old established ones. This is partly because of the character of the showman himself. While he is not averse to change he must, through

Fowler 10 h.p. Compound Showman's engine, No. 14425, "Carry On", built in 1916

financial considerations, give great thought to changing over from a ride that has proved its worth in the past to one that has yet to establish itself with the paying public. In fact, in the showman's world, there are two forms of amusements; established and novelty. The established ones are those that have proved their worth over the years. The novelty rides are the newcomers, those that require a heavy financial outlay, but which could prove to have only a limited life in the public eye. It is true that novelty rides can, over the short period when they find favour with the crowds, bring in a high return on outlay, but not all showmen want this. The majority like to see a ride bringing in a steady but regular income year in and year out, knowing that the public are unlikely to tire of a particular amusement. It is for this reason that so many of the rides that we knew in the age of steam have been carried on, possibly with alterations, to the present time. This gives the fair, even today, a character of its own. Yet few will deny that the true feeling that accompanied the old fairs can only be recaptured on the Rally field.

Unfortunately, in the beginning, many showmen appeared suspicious of the success of the Rallies and steam fairs. They saw, in the actions of

A 1919 Fowler Steam Tractor, converted to a Showman's type engine

amateurs who had the foresight to collect all the trappings of the steam era, an element of unfair competition. Many were jealous of that same foresight that saw preservationists buying old engines, often from fairground owners themselves, at scrap prices, while now these same engines changed hands for five figures.

Some of the showmen themselves, of course, kept their engines and are able, when the opportunity arises, to join in the fun of the rally, and enjoy, for a brief spell, life as they used to know it. Generally, Rallies are now being accepted by the showfolk, who will take along their own amusements or rides to add to the pleasure of the occasion.

Steam engine preservation is closely tied up with the world of the travelling showman through the only newspaper that devotes space to the preservation movement, "World's Fair". This is an institution in its own right, for not only is it one of the oldest established weekly papers, it is the only medium that gives the travelling showman news of fairs, functions and meetings in all parts of the country.

Through the "World's Fair" the showpeople can keep in touch, for its offices act as a postal address for people who are constantly moving from town to town and village to village. Each week there will be a list of letters held for the travellers, and a brief line giving their address ensures that all mail reaches them.

This then is the paper that in 1952 showed its concern for those involved in seeing that the past was not allowed to die by giving space in the paper for news of their activities. Today it carries reports of most major rallies, as well as illustrations of some of the more famous engines that put in an appearance. Through its columns owners can contact fellow owners, or even people who have an intimate knowledge of some engine through using it in its working life, and hence knowledge can be obtained that would otherwise be lost for all time.

So the Showman's Road locomotive truly deserves its place in the story of steam. Not only did it bring pleasure to countless thousands of people in the past, but today, through the medium of that remarkable newspaper, steam lives again with that greatest of all characters, the travelling fairground showman.

CHAPTER VI

Ploughing by Steam

"Iron monsters, born of necessity, that made agriculture great". Thus did one appreciative 19th century farmer describe the massive ploughing engines which, whenever they put in an appearance at the rally field today, thrill us by their sheer size and inbuilt power. Never was a tribute more deserved. For, without doubt, they were born of necessity and, even more true, it was their work on the land which first brought mechanisation into cultivation, so giving farming the impetus it needed.

The idea of using steam for land cultivation had been in the mind of man for a long time. Indeed, such a step was obvious. The farmer was previously entirely dependent on the beasts of burden - the horse and the bullock. Nothing could be hauled about the farm without them. Many realised the inherent disadvantages of these animals. They were expensive to keep, required part of the farm's own output for their support, and, like any animal, were subject to illness and death.

A mechanical counterpart seemed their logical successor. Steam, of course, was the only known power, and it was to steam that the early engineers turned to give the farmer the mechanised aid that so many called for. As early as 1814 Thomas Tindall designed a traction engine that he considered would perform adequately on the land. Alas, it was but one more item in the story of steam that failed to justify the inventor's faith.

Designed for every form of cultivation, it was a strange looking affair. For propulsion it relied on four legs which came successively in contact with the ground to give it a form of walking action. It was, so its proud builder claimed, capable of having "ploughs, harrows or even scythes attached to it". Although Tindall's idea was a failure, it did show that men were actively engaged in trying to bring steam power into general use in the field of agriculture.

The designs were many and varied. In 1822, M. J. Roberts considered a form of digger to take the place of the plough, turning over the land in the same way that a spade turns over the garden. Here, he claimed, was a more

A Fowler ploughing engine waiting for the connection to the plough to be made

efficient method of land management and one that would also show the agriculturist a financial saving. Although the idea met with scorn and abuse from many farmers, Roberts was, in fact, on the right lines. For steam diggers did, in fact, later find their way into agriculture.

However, as interesting as these early claims are, it was not until 1832 that the first real step forward was made. In that year John Heathcoat was granted a royal patent for evolving a system of agriculture cultivation using steam as the motive power. Member of Parliament for Tiverton, Heathcoat commenced work on his ideas in partnership with Josiah Parkes, consulting engineer for the Royal Agricultural Society. Parkes had spent a large part of his early engineering life involved in the drainage of bog land. Therefore when thought was given to steam cultivation, both men adapted their ideas, not basically to use on ordinary farm lands, but working and reclaiming bog land in the hope that it would become fertile, and make food production a viable proposition.

Their machine made its first appearance in 1833. Like others of the period, it was a strange contraption to look at. A flat platform supported a two cylinder steam engine, which was coupled to two winding drums. The whole was dwarfed by six massive eight foot diameter wheels, round which caterpillar tracks were fitted to enable it to traverse the boggy ground for which it was intended. In use, the idea was that the engine be positioned in the centre of the area to be worked. Ropes were then led out from the two winches, taken round pulleys positioned at either end of the field, and connected to the ends of ploughs. Further ropes joined the other end of the plough back to the winches and completed a circuit that would propel the ploughs across the fields under cultivation.

The basic idea of Heathcoat's, where the implement was drawn across a field by a stationary engine, as opposed to steam being directly harnessed to the plough, was eventually to prove the answer to the whole question of steam cultivation.

Heathcoat, however, was ahead of his time. His machine had little chance of success, and one of the great snags was the caterpillar tracks. Of necessity, Heathcoat and Parkes were forced to have them made from thin strips of iron, and the metal then available proved inadequate for their requirements. Breakdowns of the massive tracks were frequent and time wasting, but the designers had no alternative but to continue with that method.

Initially of course, both men had great faith in their creation. So much so that on 1st April, 1834, at a risk of making April Fools of themselves, they brought it out onto marshy land in Lancashire for the first tests. These were without doubt successful. The engine was driven over a mile and a half of boggy ground, and proved it could traverse the surface easily. Two years of hard work followed during which the ploughs were made, fitted with special cutting knives to hack their way through the peat and vegetation, and further modifications made to the engine itself. In 1836, it appeared again in Lancashire as a self-contained cultivating unit. Initial tests appeared to be satisfactory, but Heathcoat was not content. It had to be tried out under boggy conditions rather than on marsh land. So the whole contraption was dismantled and taken by sea to Dumfriesshire, in Scotland. There it was assembled and moved to Lochar Moss for tests before the Scottish Highland Agricultural Society. On 3rd October, 1837, a spellbound audience saw the steam cultivator working in earnest for the first time.

For more than twelve hours the two ploughs were hauled back and forth between the engine, in conditions which could hardly have been worse. For, according to one report, much of the time saw the ploughman up to his waist in water and rank vegetation. Yet, basically, that first day was a success. Over ten acres of land, previously thought unworkable, had been ploughed.

Heathcoat however, was doomed to failure through circumstances over which he had no control. The idea then prevalent was that if peat on top of bog land could be turned over successfully, the action of the weather would break down the decaying vegetation and turn it into a top soil capable of providing much needed crops. Today this is known to be wrong. Bog land is nothing more than a lake covered with growing heather and similar vegetation. The action of time on dead and decaying plants causes a top covering of peat. However, even if this is turned over and exposed to the elements, the water remains, and it is water that absorbs the chemicals required by farm crops. Heathcoat of course, was not in possession of such knowledge. He firmly believed the theories of the age and set his machine to work.

The success of the first day was to be shortlived. The press followed the proceedings with interest. Even the "Illustrated London News" gave coverage to this great happening in Scotland. Yet, even though the facts were reported, the whole thing has become cloaked in mystery. After the second day no further information was forthcoming. Nothing was said in any of the newspapers as to the final outcome. Heathcoat and his machine disappeared from public view.

Today there are two schools of thought as to its demise. Some believed that, because of its weight, it disappeared overnight in the very bog it was trying to reclaim. Others argue that Heathcoat and Parkes found some previously unknown fault that was impossible to cure. If this is so and the whole thing suddenly became impracticable it could have been abandoned in Scotland. The machine was heavy and cumbersome. To return it to its maker's yard in Lancashire would have cost a great deal of money, and Heathcoat alone had spent £12,000 on it so far. If such was the case then it could have been left to the mercy of the land it had started out with such high hopes of reclaiming.

Although unknown to him at the time, Heathcoat had pointed the pioneering finger in the direction of eventual success to others, and he had also highlighted one of the pitfalls that befell the inventor of cultivating machines. This was the fact, that with indirect ploughing the plough had to be turned by hand at the end of each run. With implements weighing up to thirteen hundredweight, and measuring nearly thirty feet in length, it was a mammoth undertaking, made even more difficult by the type of terrain that Heathcoat had intended to cultivate.

A contemporary of Heathcoate, in the field of steam ploughing, was John Upton. He however, adopted the direct approach, where the traction engine towed the cultivating implement behind it. Upton's claims for his machine were all embracing, both on the subject of efficiency and versatility. In a prospectus sent to farmers he believed would be interested, Upton claimed: "To my steam plough may be harnessed drill, seedbox or harrow and any other implement you may require to use. Its efficiency far exceeds that of the normal beast of burden. Even in the turn at the end of the furrow, my engine will give a greater area actually ploughed than any of the normal methods in use today". If this was not sufficient recommendation, Upton answered doubts about the life of the engine by saying that, "no repairs of any form should be required until after some 40,000 miles or more of actual work have been done".

Upton and Heathcoat each demonstrated the form that steam cultivation was taking. Soon there were devotees of the indirect system arguing its merits, others satisfied that only direct traction could give an efficient and capable steam plough. The eighteen years following Heathcoat's patent saw various types of engines produced for work in the fields. Each in their turn had some serious defect preventing them being applied fully to the job for which they were intended. To many it seemed that steam would never give the motive power for which the farmer was searching.

True, it was successful in the form of the portable engine in the field of threshing but no one appeared to have the ability or know-how to bring the progression forward in the manner required for practical work.

Slowly but surely a system was being evolved. In 1859 Lord Willoughby d'Eresby, on his estates at Grimsthorpe, Lincolnshire, introduced a method that followed the ideas of Heathcoat and laid the foundation which other famous names such as John Fowler, were to build on.

Lord Willoughby d'Eresby used an engine of the locomotive type, modified to include detachable drums to carry cable for indirect ploughing on the Heathcoat system. At work the engine was run on railway lines laid in the centre of the field, and the cable run out to a capstan in the headlands. The plough was worked by an endless chain some 150 yards in length. Grimsthorpe attracted many visitors to view this new system of cultivating,

Ploughing by steam. The anti-balance plough is being drawn towards an 1886 Fowler 12 h.p. engine, "Firefly"

for the owner offered his idea, unprotected by patents, for any interested party to copy.

Figures issued at the time said that the system could do the work of sixteen normal ploughs using anything up to thirty or more horses. Only eight men, and one horse and water cart to fetch water for the engine, were required. The saving in manpower alone was one hundred per cent. Unlike many others, who, after primary tests seemed to drop out of the fight for perfection, Lord Willoughby d'Eresby, worked his system in rural Lincolnshire for the next five years. Yet the answer, for steam ploughing, when it came, surprisingly enough brought into service that already established farm machine, the portable.

Portables were used in agriculture in their thousands. The tasks they performed were many and diverse, but two factors affected their efficiency. Firstly they still needed horses for motive power, and secondly their uses were limited. For long periods they would stand unused. The man who used his genius to change the portable from just an engine used at harvest time and for odd jobs round the farm, to a truly universal farm implement was a farmer named Hannam, from Burcote, near Abingdon in Berkshire. His ingenuity saw a new piece of equipment enter the story – the "windlass". Briefly this consisted of two independent drums mounted on a wheeled base. The drums, belt driven from the farm portable, provided the circular motion to let out and take in a cable to a plough in a similar manner to that used by Heathcoat and at the Grimsthorpe Estates. With the addition of just one piece of extra equipment and cable, the farmer had not only a complete ploughing system, but the means to extend the use of the portable engine during periods when it would otherwise be standing idle.

This idea of Hannam, which was used successfully until the introduction of the great pairs of ploughing engines, became known as the "roundabout system". In use, a free running rope of iron wire was taken round the field to be ploughed, through guide pulleys positioned in the corners. The engine was coupled by a belt to the windlass, which in turn was linked to the rope. This could now run from the windlass, round the field and back, hence making a complete circuit. The plough, which in those early days was a normal horse drawn plough, was incorporated at one edge.

There were drawbacks. Several farm workers were needed to move the pulleys after each crossing, as the area still to be ploughed narrowed, but it had the great advantage of providing any farmer owning a portable engine with a ploughing system at little extra cost. Hannam's windlass was built for him by a firm of Reading engineers, but when the merits were proved, outside manufacturers began to enter the field offering complete sets of ploughing tackle.

Another farmer who made a name for himself with the "windlass system" was William Smith, from Little Woolstone, Buckinghamshire. He placed an order with Howard Bros., Engineers of Bedford, to construct not only a windlass, but a cultivator to his own design. Coupled to a Ransome portable, the cultivator, by reversing the direction of the drums on the windlass, could be drawn backwards and forwards across the field.

The popularity of the "roundabout" system can be seen from the fact that, at the 1851 Great Exhibition, Hornsby, Burrell, Ransome and May, Tuxford, Shuttleworth and Garrett were but a few of the firms offering this idea to the farmer.

Indeed, by 1862 no less than two hundred sets modelled on the "Smith System" had been supplied by Howards to contented customers. The 1850's of course, are notable for the emergence of the man who became synonymous with every aspect of steam ploughing - John Fowler. Born at Melksham in Wiltshire in 1826 into a fairly wealthy Quaker family, he commenced his working life in a country corn business.

His heart however, was in engineering, and on coming of age he moved to the Middlesbrough firm of Gilkes, Wilson and Hopkins who were making among other things, steam locomotives. In 1849, at the age of 23, John Fowler took a holiday in Ireland. This event was to change his whole life. At the time of his visit the country was suffering the aftermath of the terrible potato blight of 1846-7. Fowler was horrified at the hardship and deprivations of the starving country folk. His horror was made even greater when he saw the vast areas of uncultivated land which, with adequate drainage, could provide the life-giving food that Ireland needed so badly.

On his return to England he devoted his time and energies to perfecting a form of a mole draining plough similar to one experimented with earlier by a man called Saul in Lancashire. At the Royal Show in 1850, John Fowler demonstrated his first mole plough to the farmers in the Exeter area. It was designed to lay wooden pipes to a depth of two feet in heavy clay soil. At this stage he had not considered steam as a form of motive power, and this early implement was worked by either men or horses turning a capstan positioned at the end of the field.

Fowler knew however, of the hard work involved and soon his mind had turned to the idea of steam.

At Lincoln, in 1854, John Fowler showed for the first time a draining plough with anchors and windlass driven by a Clayton and Shuttleworth portable steam engine. So successful was the equipment that he received one of the top prizes awarded at the show.

Fowler of course, was using the basic system that Hannam and Smith used for steam cultivating, so there is small wonder that his mind turned to this form of work after his successes with the mole plough. There was, at that time, a prize offered by the Royal Agricultural Society of England, for the

Close-up of the winding drum on a Fowler cultivating engine, showing the wire rope used to haul in the plough

first truly proved system of steam cultivation that could be used on land at a more economical and efficient rate than the old time honoured methods then in use. John Fowler determined to win that prize.

He was soon experimenting with the "roundabout system". But it was a chance meeting with a Scottish farmer, David Greig, then living in Essex, that brought his eventual success. So impressed was Fowler by Greig's grasp of the problems involved in steam ploughing, that he offered him a job as technical advisor. Greig rapidly proved his worth. The two men, working together, designed a plough specially for steam working. Prior to this, the old horse drawn types had, of necessity, to be used, with the inherent disadvantage that the shares faced only one direction.

In 1856, Greig and Fowler took out a patent for a balance plough, which consisted of two sets of four shares. One set was left handed and the other right handed. In use one set of shares was dropped in the ground and the other set rode up in the air. On the completion of one pull across the field, all that was required was for the airborne shares to be dropped in the ground, the others raised, and the plough was ready for the return crossing without having to be reversed.

This plough was the basis of all future balance and anti-balance ploughs, that were to form an integral part of steam ploughing through its entire lifetime.

Fowler's system was similar to that already in use. A double drum windlass was connected by means of a belt to a portable engine. Then a cable from one drum was run out round a pulley, across to another anchor pulley, and thus in a straight line down the field to be worked, to the plough. The cable from the other drum was fed, again through an anchor pulley, to the other end of the plough. In use, as one drum pulled the plough across in one direction, the other drum could pull in the reverse direction. With the addition of the balance plough the system was improved one hundred per cent.

In 1858 Fowler achieved his first ambition. The prize for the first economical steam plough gear had been increased to £500. It was awarded to him at the R.A.S.E. Show at Chester.

The following year saw Fowler clearly beginning to show his supremacy in the field of steam cultivation, for at the Royal Show his three and four furrow balance ploughs proved their worth over every other type entered.

Up to then Fowler had suffered from the same disadvantage that had plagued Aveling in his early days – the lack of works in which his ideas could be developed by craftsmen under his direct control, for his manufacturing work had been done either by Clayton and Shuttleworth, Ransome and Sims or by Fry of Bristol.

However, in 1859, Fowler realised that if steam ploughing was to succeed, engines of greater power than those then available were urgently needed. He tackled the problems in a typical Fowler manner and formed the "Steam Plough Royalty Company Ltd". His friends and relatives were invited to invest, in return for profits in the future. It is interesting to recall that this was one of the earliest joint stock companies to be formed. So Fowler could possibly claim yet another "first" to add to his other triumphs. By 1860 finance was complete, and he was at last able to open his own manufacturing works at Hunslet, Leeds.

He had already experimented with a system of ploughing by means of two engines, one stationed at either end of the field, and with a balance plough pulled between them. The advantage of the system was the doing away with the need for anchor pulleys, but the disadvantage, in the eyes of many farmers and land owners, was the need for two engines. It was, however, a two engine system that left his works in 1861 as the first proud creation of the "Steam Plough Works" of John Fowler. These twin engine sets were, of course, different in appearance from the earlier engines used in the round-about system.

The cable drum was now slung horizontally below the boiler as an integral part of the engine. The windlass of course, had now been done away with and the ploughing engine was a self contained entirety. The system however, could be adapted to "roundabout" working and for this purpose, Fowler built and sold an engine with double drums fitted. One was used to haul in the cable as the other let it out and the positions reversed for the return haul. Alas, none of this particular type has survived but, thanks to the patience of the model builder, at least one scale model prepared from actual works drawings can be seen at steam meetings illustrating the system that Fowler perfected using a single engine.

The year 1861 saw yet another innovation. Fowler adopted a system known as the "Clip or Burton" drums as used on coal mine pithead cages, for the winding drums of his engines. The advantages here centred mainly round the hinged jaws that closed round the cable under stress and held it firmly in their grip, without the need for it to pass a number of times round the drum.

By 1863, Fowler and steam ploughing were firmly established in the country as a whole. At the Smithfield Show that year, a pair of Fowler ploughing engines of completely new design drew admiration from all who visited it. Rated at 10 n.h.p., they followed what is now accepted design and broke away completely from the old portable style. Fowler however, did not live to enjoy the glory. Overwork had reduced him to a poor state of health, and on medical advice he moved to the village of Ackworth, outside Leeds, and began a period of recuperation, living the life of a country gentleman. Horse riding was one of his favourite pastimes and he now devoted as much time to it as possible. Alas, it was this that caused his end. Out foxhunting in November, 1864, he was thrown from his horse and seriously injured his arm. Despite the best medical care, blood poisoning set in and on the 4th December, the man who had finally established steam ploughing as á practical proposition, passed away at the early age of thirty-eight.

No better description of the position at the time of Fowler's death can be obtained than from literature of that period which records:

"Fowler's steam ploughing apparatus is made according to four different systems, each with its own advantages. In the first there are two engines, one of which is positioned on either side of the field to be ploughed and the implement is drawn between them. This has the disadvantage of increased cost, but with the advantages that the engines can themselves draw the necessary tackle and once at the scene of operations can be quickly set in motion.

"In the second system there is only one engine positioned at one side of the field, while on the other there is an anchor which forms the point of resistance for the steel rope that pulls the plough. This anchor is a sort of heavy carriage with a horizontal wheel round which the cable turns, and resting on four thin disc wheels which sink into the ground and prevent the anchor being dragged sideways by the force of the rope, but on which it may move forwards when necessary.

"In the third system the apparatus is constructed so that it may be worked in the same way as the second system, or with the engine stationed in one corner of the field, snatch blocks being used to guide the cable to and from the plough. In the fourth system the engine is also stationed in the corner of the field and the ploughing implement is drawn between two anchors on opposite sides of the field. This ploughing implement has several shares for different furrows. It is likewise always double, having similar sets of shares before and behind, and is so constructed that when one set of shares is in the ground, the other is high in the air. This arrangement obviates the necessity of turning. As steam ploughing tackle is usually beyond the means and the requirements of single farmers, companies have been formed at various places to hire them out to all who want them".

This later statement is of course, a follow on to the threshing contràctor. As steam ploughing became established and the system of plough engines at either side of the field gained ascendancy, the cost made it uneconomical for most farmers to use their own engines. The contractor came into his own in this field. So to agriculture John Fowler gave steam ploughing as it evolved over the years, through Heathcoat's experiments, Hannam and Smith's ingenuity, to bear fruit in his own genius. But what would the future be now that John Fowler had passed from the scene? Expansion or stagnation?

CHAPTER VII

The End of Steam Cultivation

Fortunately for the future of steam cultivation, John Fowler, as well as being a brilliant design engineer, had the ability to select and build a team around him capable of the same dedication that he himself gave to the task in hand.

After his tragic death, the Hunslet works were reorganised bringing David Greig, the brains behind the balance plough, into the business as a partner with direct responsibliity for technical design. The commercial side of the work was undertaken by John Fowler's brother, Robert.

Both men had a good foundation from which to embark on even bigger and better ploughing engines. At the time of this upheaval in management, the "Steam Plough Works" employed no less than 600 people, and one machine was rolling out of the factory gates each week. That such numbers were needed for the production of these old steamers shows in part the reason why, even today, many have survived the rigours of a working life to live on and grace our summer scene, as resplendent as the day they left the works.

It was shortly after the death of the founder that the Hunslet works introduced the engines that could be said to be the predecessors of those we see today. These were Fowler's horizontal shaft "steamers". The drive to the winding drum fitted below the boiler was now by means of a horizontal shaft and bevel gearing meshing, with the crankshaft at one end and the drum drive shaft at the other. This is the feature that became standard on the great cultivators, and during their entire working life no better system was discovered.

The output from the Hunslet works settled into a definite pattern, with their machines following specified classifications. The "K" series were light h.p. engines; the "B.4's" were 8 h.p.; the "A.A's" a more powerful 12 h.p.; and the "Z's" 14 h.p. By 1914 however there was a need for yet another engine. In the farming world the cultivator was finding favour in place of the plough, and an engine was required that would allow it to be drawn across the field faster than when the balance plough was used.

So the "B.B" class came into being through a higher rope speed, increasing

A close-up of the drum gear of a Fowler ploughing engine

work from the 4 m.p.h. of the plough to the required 6 m.p.h. for the cultivator. It is mainly these "B.B" engines that have survived through to today to demonstrate their ability and working power at Rallies.

Whenever we speak of steam cultivation our minds turn to John Fowler and his magnificent engines, but he was not the only man producing these work-horses of the countryside. Steam was never the prerogative of one man. Other manufacturers followed in his footsteps and turned out ploughing engines that performed equally well. Some names, such as the Oxfordshire Steam Ploughing Company, are today almost forgotten, but in their time they produced machines which, in the eyes of many, were equal if not superior to Fowlers.

This company came into the Manufacture of ploughing engines almost by accident. In a rural area where steam cultivation was firmly established, they began as makers of replacement parts for Fowler's engines, and others brought to them for repair. Gradually modifications were made to engines until, in 1908 they brought out their own design. It was economical and efficient and found a ready market in the Oxfordshire area. Economy of both

The six furrow type anti-balance plough

water and coal were matters of the greatest importance, particularly on farms where even water had to be hauled long distances to keep the ploughing engines at work. Hence, when these new machines showed a saving on fuel, farmers readily invested in them at the expense of the more well known makes.

As the Oxfordshire Steam Ploughing Company came into the manufacturing side accidentally, so the well known firm of Charles Burrell turned its attention to this side of steam almost apologetically. The firm's interest, as opposed to Fowler's early specialisation in cultivating, covered a wide range of traction engines, from portables through general purpose to road haulage machines. Steam ploughing, however, was not entirely neglected. In conjuction with the Norfolk engineers Everitt and Adams they adapted a system perfected by Everitt, whereby the winding drum was fitted on the right hand side of the engine in an upright position. These were built as either left or right hand machines for double ploughing work, or with two drums on one engine for use in roundabout work.

Although John Fowler gained ascendency in cultivation, other makers did not bow entirely to his undoubted advances. J & F Howard of Bedford, whose name has already been mentioned, looked at one time as if they could become serious rivals to Fowler in the fight for supremacy. Although it had been proved that the system with the winding drum slung horizontally below the boiler was the best possible one for steam cultivation, Howards persisted in experimenting with other means.

Their ideas, compared with the conventional engines we know today, appeared weird and wonderful. Their traverse boiler ploughing engine of 1867 had, as its name implies, the boiler traverse across the engine, with the huge winding drum mounted vertically behind it, also traverse, from which the cable was let out to the implements to be worked.

Other engines had the winding drum mounted at the rear, also in a vertical position, with a pulley horizontally mounted under the boiler to feed the cable to the implement and ensure a smooth pull.

This type of engine, known as the "Farmer's Friend" was without doubt their most successful, particularly so because the drums could be removed when the engine became a normal traction engine suitable for use in threshing. Thus, Howard's intention was to provide one engine that could do every job needing power around the farm. The idea was a bold one but it never caught on with users as did Fowler's methods.

Other names have also added to this chapter of steam. Aveling and Porter of Rochester followed the Fowler system with their engines and, in fact, the two firms at one time co-operated with patents granted to Fowler for steam work. Tuxford and Sons of Boston, Lincolnshire; Savage Bros of King's Lynn; and Marshall and Sons of Gainsborough, Lincolnshire, were others who ventured into steam cultivating, but hardly enough to worry the Fowler combine. The same cannot be said of J. and H. McLaren of Leeds who, although late starters, building their first ploughing engine in 1876, soon established a reputation. In appearance their engines were similar to the Leeds stable-mate made at Fowler's. In every respect they were their equals, both in reliability and ease of working. Soon they were exporting to Europe and beyond. If the firm had entered the field earlier and had someone with the brilliance of John Fowler as design engineer, there is no doubt that they would have taken over the leading place in the story of steam ploughing.

All these firms, however, added to an output of machines which brought into being one of the best known agricultural businesses – the steam plough contractors. Financial requirements for pairs of engines for the double plough syestem and their ancilliary implements were high. Hence, ploughing contractors invested large sums of money in equipment that could be hired out at rates showing a good return on capital investment.

Their names became household words in the countryside as their engines lumbered from farm to farm. Names such as the West Riding Steam

The anti-balance plough. The six shares were an effective and quick method of ploughing

Ploughing and Threshing Company; the Gloucestershire Steam Plough Company; and the Eddison Steam Ploughing Company of Dorchester rolled off the tongues of country people with the familiarity associated with present day car firms. Each in its own way did much to make steam cultivation the success that it became and, to show how they lived and worked, one can do no better than delve into the records of Ward and Dale, a firm from Sleaford, Lincolnshire.

This was one of the most famous of the old contractors, and was almost certainly flourishing in the 1880's. In 1910 it became a limited company, with assets including ploughing engines valued at over £15,000. The firm was known not only in Lincolnshire, but Nottinghamshire, Leicestershire, Rutland and even Northamptonshire, where the pairs of massive Fowler engines used to work during the ploughing and cultivating season. In fact, during 1914, nearly 65,000 acres of land were cultivated by Ward and Dale. The season lasted from April to December, when the firm payed off the workers until the next year. Some of the men took casual agricultural work, but others lived during the days of unemployment on the money earned during the working months.

Each pair of engines needed a crew of five: two engine drivers, a steersman

A demonstration to show how the cultivator was used with the two engine system

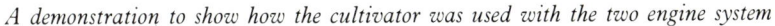

for the massive plough, the foreman in overall charge of the work, and a boy, usually straight from school, who acted as cook and general labourer. The work was hard and the hours long. When a farmer was paying by the acre, he rarely allowed any slacking from the contractors. The equipment was expected to keep working even through meal times. When the "boy cook" signalled that the mixture of boiled bacon and potatoes was ready, each man in turn would "wine and dine", using the foreman as relief crew man.

Ploughing or cultivating started at first light and went on until it was too dark to possibly continue. Then the tired crews would collapse in their bunks in the living wagon they towed from job to job, more often than not fully dressed. Some weekends saw them returning home late on Saturday, but one man at least had to be back with the engines to light the fires by 4 a.m. on Monday so that steam would be up and work could commence immediately the others arrived on the scene.

Life for these men was hard and their wages poor. The only concession they received was a bonus on the amount of acreage covered, and this was witheld by the firm until work was over for the season. With this, the more careful could survive financially until the following year. .

While the ploughing engines do, of course, thrill and excite us today, what of the implements themselves? The basis of steam ploughing by the direct method was the balance plough. The disadvantage with this type was the fact

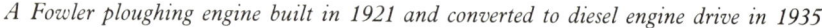

A Fowler ploughing engine built in 1921 and converted to diesel engine drive in 1935

that it was balanced in the centre. This made it easy for the crews to effect a change of direction, but during hard pulling on light land this very act of balance gave a tendency for the working end to lift out of the ground.

Fowler's answer was the anti-balance plough. In appearance identical with the balance plough, the anti-balance was so designed that on the first pull the wheels moved forward from the point of balance and ensured that the working back end could not lift up during ploughing.

This anti-balance gear consisted of rollers working along guide rails and was so arranged that as the plough took the first strain on the rope, so the wheels were moved forward and the back end dropped firmly into the ground. At the end of the run, as the rope tension was released, so the wheels came back to their central position, pivoting the plough on its point of balance for ease of manhandling.

With either five or six shares, this became the standard implement in England during the days of steam ploughing. It was pulled across the field at a speed of between three and four miles per hour. Any higher speed had been

A powerful Fowler cultivating engine, built in 1886. The winding drum can be clearly seen beneath the boiler

shown to have an adverse effect on the quality of the ploughing.

Yet the anti-balance plough was never a really efficient tool. Its use on stubble or land that had a heavy crop of thistles or other weeds, the ploughing was never a clean job. At the conclusion of the work the stubble and weeds were not completely buried, as required by a farmer wanting maximum value for his money. New ideas were sought and the cultivator began to gain ascendancy over the plough.

The cultivator, therefore, became the main implement, and the term "steam ploughing" was replaced by "steam cultivating". In the later years of service this in fact is what the "steamers" were mainly engaged on. A three wheel turning cultivator, known in many parts of the country as the "Grubber" because of the action of its tines, was the most famous of all steam implements. Cultivators varied in size, with a giant fitted with eleven tines capable of turning over forty acres of land in one working day.

Usually steam cultivators worked on the "Done & Crossed" system, whereby a field was torn up by the tines in one direction, then they were pulled across a second time, crossing the previous direction of work. The great advantage of this implement was its ability to break up the heavy, hard clay land in summer, and expose weeds etc. to the killing rays of the sun, as well as exposing the earth itself to the action of the weather.

Work usually started after the harvest, when stubble land was fully prepared for the fallow period. Often the same field was done twice in one summer. Early in June the cultivators would expose the soil to the action of the sun. Then, possibly during August, they would revisit and turn over any weeds that may have escaped during the previous visit.

Cultivators did not, of course, entirely displace the plough. In fact, during the period when steam predominated in this form of work, Fowler's alone offered no less than seven hundred different variations of their basic plough. Many were specially designed for overseas markets where the land differed from that in Great Britain. Whatever the type of land, Fowler's could ensure that the most effective arrangement of mole boards and shares were fitted to that particular anti-balance plough.

Other implements were also available from a wide range of manufacturers. These varied through the harrow and field roller, to a combined seed drill and harrow. Mole ploughs, the first implement made by Fowler, found service in areas of marshy and wet land, where they represented both an efficient and cheap method of draining the fields.

Even dredging was within the capabilities of the steam plough engines, and many lakes and reservoirs were dredged with a huge bucket hauled along the bottom of the lake by ploughing engines. In fact this system still exists, and many believe that for efficiency and ease it has never been equalled. Only recently two such engines could be seen performing this task near Warsop in

Nottinghamshire. Alas in this case the old tell-tale spiral of smoke that marked the steamers in the days of old was missing. Progress had overtaken them, and the once proud engines had suffered the indignity of conversion to diesel power. With that conversion seemed to have gone the pride that the old engine men had in their machines. Here was none of the affection and care that kept ploughing engines in mint condition, but rather rust and decay were very much evident. Yet it is a tribute to those engineers of long ago that at least they were still capable of doing the work they were first intended for.

Although steam was now firmly established and the original idea of steam ploughing had extended its boundaries, there was a dark cloud on the horizon.

As early as 1892 the Chase Steam Company in America had experimented with a direct pull tractor powered by the internal combustion engine. At first it seemed to offer no threat to established methods. However, just as Fowler had fought and worked to bring steam into land cultivation, so his successors, in their turn, began to make their own experiments in this new form of power.

A Fowler 14 h.p. single cylinder ploughing engine supplied new in 1873

By 1909 the petrol or diesel tractor was making its appearance at Agricultural Shows alongside the steam engines it was later to displace. Steam in the form of indirect cultivation had no answer to these small and cheaper methods of mechanical power. Indirect cultivation, however, had always had its critics: men who believed that the true use of steam in cultivation lay in the direct methods with either the implement being towed by the engine or even fitted directly to it.

The trouble, in the past, had always been the weight of the engine itself. Even under good conditions on firm land such was the pressure transmitted to the soil that it packed it down and made the work of the plough being pulled even more difficult. Yet, in face of this new competition, direct traction tried again.

In 1917 Richard Garrett & Co., of Leiston put on the market their "Suffolk Punch" direct steam tractor, named after the shire horse that had made the county so famous. It was an abortive attempt to ward off the inevitable as was the attempt by Mann and Co. who produced a similar direct traction steam engine. The end was in sight. Steam had come full circle through the work of Heathcoat, Fowler and now Garrett and Mann. The internal combustion

A 1918 Garrett Suffolk Punch Tractor, No. 33180, built to fight the menace of the tractor, as the end of steam approached

engined tractor was here to stay. Yet despite their efficiency and usefulness as the complete farm tool, tractors lacked character in the eyes of many. Their history can never compare with the thrilling story of steam. For steam truly had its brave experimentors: men who were prepared to withstand the scorn that others, often less enlightened, would direct against them. It is fitting as the story of steam cultivation sadly comes to an end, to consider just one more person in that epic struggle for supremacy.

Thomas Churchill Derby was a small engineer with premises in the Essex village of Pleshy near Chelmsford. Yet although his premises were small, his outlook was not. Derby never faltered in his belief that others were wrong, and only by reverting to the time honoured system of digging the land could maximum value be got from steam. He set to work to prove theories that in the past had been ridiculed, and by 1878 he was ready to demonstrate his ideas.

On the land to be worked the machine dispensed with wheels and relied on a walking action by metal legs to take it sideways across the field. Six four-tined forks were arranged to move in and out of the ground in sequence. As it moved on its clumsy legs the machine left behind an eighteen feet wide area that had been turned over to a depth of about nine inches.

The Garrett Suffolk Punch demonstrating its work

Despite drawbacks, Derby persisted and both McLaren and Savage made diggers to his specification. Gradually he improved on the action, and by the end of 1891 had built or had built for him no less than thirty machines, the price of which had dropped from the original £1000 plus to a mere £600. Although never popular in the same sense as other forms of steam cultivation, people did buy and use these strange machines, and some in fact backed up the maker's theory that this was the most effective system of cultivation available.

Derby, therefore made yet another piece of history in the story of steam, and added his name to the pioneers who were prepared to back up their theories with practical work.

Even today there are farmers who agree that, in basic outline, Derby's system was without doubt the one to give maximum benefit to the land. However, like many other ideas, the digger has never encouraged the big manufacturers to persist with its development, so we shall never know if Derby was in fact on the right lines.

The evolution of the internal combustion engine, of course, sounded the death knell for the ploughing contractors. The farmer could now afford to

An example of direct ploughing with a Manns, 4 h.p. compound Tractor No. 1425

buy a small and cheap tractor that would do all the work he had previously paid outsiders to do.

Some firms surrendered early, like T. B. Kitchener of Potton, Bedfordshire, who went into voluntary liquidation in 1927. Others tried to carry on. Ward and Dale were among the latter, but the going became hard. Sets of cultivators had to be reduced as work decreased. Often they were sold for mere scrap value. A sad end indeed for such loved and hard working equipment that had brought the firm to the position of prominence they attained during the heyday of steam cultivation.

By 1930 the tractor had almost completely taken over from steam. It was said, by a prominent agriculturalist of the time, that an internal combustion caterpillar tractor with a six furrow plough could turn over ten acres in one day. The steam cultivator could boast of twelve acres in one day. But, the steam method relied on an least five men, while the tractor could be operated by a single workman.

A Fowler six furrow balance plough working with a pair of compound Fowler steam ploughing engines

Ward and Dale stuck it out to the bitter end. They reduced the price charged to the farmer, but this only resulted in the firm actually losing money; a commercial fact that no concern could live with.

By 1938 they had virtually no work, and on 10th March, 1939 all their tackle came under the auctioneer's hammer. Nor was it a profitable sale. Few people could see steam ploughing engines attaining any of their former use or value. If only those present had been able to foresee the state of the preservation movement as it is today, and the price that a pair of Fowler Class BB's would fetch if put on offer.

Then of course the position was different. In all, ten ploughing sets were sold. With the exception of a pair of "AA" engines, all were "BB's". The highest price realised was £140. The lowest a mere £50 for a pair of engines. Ploughs did not even reach £10, while cultivators did little better. It was indeed a sad day for those old men of steam who witnessed the sale.

It is true that some farmers, in a mood of nostalgia, bought ploughing engines at various sales up and down the country, and still used them for a decade or more on their own land, employing existing labour to recreate a method they had grown up with and longed to preserve. Progress, however, is inevitable. Even enthusiasts eventually moved to diesel, and today old ploughing engines remain only in the hands of preservationists. Through their efforts we can again stand in the presence of the one time greats and marvel, through their development, at the work of Heathcoat, Hannam and Smith, and at the genius of John Fowler.

CHAPTER VIII

The Mighty Steam Wagon

The 1896 Locomotive Act had, indeed, far reaching consequences. Free from previous restrictive influences, designers and engineers could turn their attention to the development of steam as a form of road transport.

Road locomotives became a common sight, but the use of steam for general haulage went even further. Although these engines served their purpose admirably when it came to the haulage of heavy trailers, they had their disadvantages. In themselves they were incapable of carrying goods, and were both slow and cumbersome, particularly in narrow country roads. So men turned their minds back to the early days of steam development, when they saw in this form of motive power, not the means to produce the work horse of the countryside, but rather a means whereby passengers and goods could be taken from place to place, widening the boundaries of the whole country. It was an idea that produced one of the most attractive vehicles that can be seen at a modern traction engine rally – the steam wagon.

The traction engine as we know it is missing from their design. Here is the identifiable forerunner of the modern motor lorry and motor car of today. The driving cab, the long load carrying base and, above all, road wheels of the type that we ourselves have become familiar with, are all incorporated.

These steam wagons have a charm and appeal that can never be equalled by the petrol or diesel engine vehicle. Their reliability became a byword in an age accustomed to the excellence of engineering. Their sheer grace leaves one with nothing but admiration, but I believe that their appeal lies even deeper than this. Here is truly a vanished age. The age of the small shopkeeper, when men took pride in their trade, and customers were acknowledged with reverence and their wishes respected on every occasion.

To visit a Rally and walk round the assembled wagons is truly to turn back the pages of history. For not only is each one sure to be restored to its original condition, but gaily painted with details of the owner's name, address and also his business.

Their evolution, as has been said, was a logical follow on from man's early thoughts about possible uses for steam. Yet though their progress was retarded by the prohibitive legislation that marred the early days of steam, in one way it could have been an advantage.

Beause of the attitude of authority, those with beliefs in the future of steam were forced to leave all ideas of passenger transport to the railways, and give their undivided attention to its use as a general work horse. The result was the evolution of the traction engine to the machine of near perfection that it became.

If, on the other hand, men had a free hand to use steam without let or hindrance, then it is possible that their efforts would have been divided. Many would have concentrated on road transport to the exclusion of all else, leaving but a mere handful to follow steam into the countryside. If either set had proved to be in the lower divisions as designers and engineers, both aspects could have failed.

As it was, when 1898 saw the beginning of the end of restrictions, steam was already established and those experienced in one form, could now turn their attention to this new mode. This accumulated knowledge of traction engine design saw a range of steam wagons come onto the market that made

A Yorkshire Two Ton Wagon No. 117, built in 1905
and restored to its original perfection

Britain supreme in this field. Although other countries turned their attention to this form of commercial vehicle, none approached the design perfection or mechanical excellence that was the hallmark of Britain's products.

The first steam wagon builder, however, came before this time. As early as 1875 the firm of Brown and May, in Devizes, Wiltshire, produced such a vehicle for local use. Unfortunately today we have no knowledge of the system used, but without doubt it was based on their successful line of traction engines.

If little is now known of these Wiltshire builders, the same cannot be said for the next man to try his luck. When young James Sumner, a steam enthusiast from Leyland, Lancashire, made a 5 ton wagon to carry coal from local pits to Stanning's Bleach Works in the town in 1884, it was the start of a line that has continued through to this day. Wherever motor cars or commercial vehicles are discussed, the name "Leyland" stands for excellence and reliability.

In those early days, though, its maker had to rely on the financial backing of the factory owner, William Stanning, until fate took a hand.

Standing for election to the local County Council, Stanning found, to his surprise, that his Liberal opponent was fighting the election on the grounds that steam wagons were a danger to life and limb, and a menace on the roads to every law abiding citizen. In the prevailing climate of those days, with Stanning's faith in steam common knowledge, it was his opponent who won. In the end Stanning decided he could do more good for the future of road transport if securely established on the Council, and his active support of James Sumner was withdrawn. So the steam wagon started its last journey from its home to Ormskirk and back. The journey however, was not without mishap. For, although Sumner took his young brother along to act as the "red flag boy", the journey took no less than four days, with part of the time being spent in a Magistrates' Court pleading guilty to a summons in which the police alleged that he did "willfully leave one locomotive unattended on the highway".

The fact that this occurred on a Saturday night and in a place where no-one could harm themselves on it, or that the reason was a mechanical breakdown, made no difference. Steam drivers who broke the law, however inadvertantly, could expect no mercy. So the wagon ended its life ingloriously with the body being scrapped and the engine finishing its working life driving a saw bench.

Sumner, however, was far from finished. When in 1892 he inherited the family engineering works, he turned his attention to producing steam lawn mowers. Although a far cry from his lorry design, they were so successful that he cleared his business debts and accumulated sufficient capital for future development.

A 1932 Sentinel type D.G.4 two speed wagon, used for tar spraying until 1956

Then in 1896 came the relaxation of the law that had caused his earlier failure and he wasted no time in putting his plans into operation. With a partner, Henry Spurrier, he formed the Lancashire Steam Motor Company. The first model to leave his Leyland works was a 30 cwt van powered by a vertical oil fired boiler driving a two cylinder compound engine developing some 14 h.p. The final drive was applied to the rear axle through a three speed gear box and friction clutches.

Next to follow was a three ton truck, and although both models found ready markets, guided by customer reaction, the Leyland works had soon turned from oil to coal fired boilers. With the 4 ton model "B" wagon there was a working pressure of 2,000 lbs per square inch, an engine developing 35 h.p. and two speed gears driving the road wheels through a shaft and chain. Progress was rapid. By 1902 a new factory had been opened and soon no less than forty steam wagons had left the production line, including a fleet of Leylands for the Road Carrying Company of Liverpool.

1917 "Pendle Queen" in use until 1931. This example is unique in the rally field having the horizontal boiler mounted transversely on the chassis

Yet Leyland was not the only firm in this new field. With the passing of a final restrictions on road haulage, development had followed along two distinct paths. Firstly, established traction engine manufacturers such as Robey, Fowler, Burrell, Clayton and Shuttleworth and Wallis and Stevens turned their undoubted talents to this form of locomotion. Secondly, firms without direct knowledge of traction engine building entered the field. Sumner and his Leyland works was one. Others were Thorneycroft, Sentinel, and the Yorkshire Patent Steam Wagon Company.

While this form of work may have been new to them, none were new to steam. Thorneycrofts had experience dating back to 1865, with a successful and highly profitable range of steam launches. The Yorkshire Patent Steam Wagon Company had, for its foundations, an interest in steam derived from other sources. As a branch of Deighton's Patent Flue and Tube Company Ltd., it was brought into being to develop a steam wagon incorporating the Yorkshire double ended locomotive type boiler, an aim which was achieved with excellence. From the beginning, the steam wagon succeeded in every direction.

By 1897 Thorneycroft had built a "Tip Wagon" for municipal work with the Chiswick Urban District Council. Chelsea and Wandsworth Councils, in their turn, bought fleets of Leyland vehicles. Thorneycroft further distinguished themselves when a government contract was placed for steam wagons for service in the South African War under Lord Kitchener.

Yet, by 1904 the writing was on the wall, and the first message came from within the steam builders own ranks. Leyland, in that year, built an internal combustion engined wagon. Although it was a failure, the company continued experimenting with petrol engines until, by 1910 they were able to offer a buyer the choice of petrol or steam.

No-one was better qualified than Leylands to compare the two systems. "Petrol", they said, "was superior when carrying loads of less than four tons. From four to six tons there is nothing between the two. Above that figure, and for the haulier with daily mileages of less than fifty, steam is far more economical taking into account the cost of petrol". So depending on the type of work undertaken, at this point, steam and petrol could live side by side with each other.

Yet there were inherent drawbacks to the steam wagon. The vertical boilered engines were not fully efficient steamers, with a notable power loss. For this reason Foden's took the first step when they turned their attention to what became a typically British feature – the overtype engine.

Here a short locomotive type boiler was fitted with the working motions mounted on top. Although of increased efficiency, the great disadvantage was that the length of the boiler and cab cut down the load carrying capacity unless a very long wheel base was fitted. Despite this, it dominated the steam

Close-up of the front of the Foden "Overtype", showing the badge signifying the "Royal Appointment" of Fodens Ltd

wagon field for over twenty years. Fodens never lost the initial grip they had taken, but many other manufacturers followed their lead. Yet, when commerce began to find its feet in the 1920's, and firms became cost conscious, the reduction in load carrying capacity, as compared with the vertical type boiler, sounded its death knell.

The vertical boilered wagons with the engine slung beneath the chassis were made for a much greater load carrying ability which, in the field of general haulage was what attracted the buyer. So it was this type, with which the story of the steam wagon began, that saw it through to the end of its era.

In the field of the undertype, Sentinel stood supreme. They had remained faithful to it from the start, and how they must have laughed as those who had followed Foden's example rapidly turned back to this system. Indeed, so

A Foden "Overtype" of 1926. This example had three speeds and was originally used as a three way tipper on the Essex roads

successful were the first Sentinel designs, that they stood the company in good stead until the early 1920's. Then, in 1923, they consolidated the lead they held with a twin cylinder undertype, the "Super Sentinel". Yet, with all their technical advantages of design, the firm stayed with the single speed wagon, despite its limitations when compared with the multi-geared vehicles.

By 1927, however, they had to acknowledge their mistake and so produced a two speed model. This was rapidly followed by a six wheel truck. And, if the commercial world marvelled at this, they were further astounded when, in the early 1930's Sentinel introduced a steam wagon with four steerable wheels at the front and four drive wheels at the rear. The end, nevertheless was rapidly approaching. Buyers were turning from steam to the internal combustion engine.

Even an invitation to Doble, the great steam designer, to come to England and work on an entirely new form of steam wagon, could not halt the inevitable. Experimental work on the Sentinel-Doble vehicle actually got under way, but before it reached the production lines the firm had to face and accept the change progress was bringing.

No mention of steam wagons can be complete without a look at the achievements of the Yorkshire Patent Steam Wagon Company, whose very name, surely, has a ring of mystery and romance about it. Their vehicles were distinguished by the traverse boiler undertype engines and today, among a gathering of steam wagons, the design stands out from others. It speaks volumes for the general reliability of their designs, that this was another firm whose initial vehicles survived for many years with little change or modification.

From the beginning the Yorkshire patent double-ended engine was brought into service, with drive to the rear axle by gearing through a two speed box, and although many types of bodies were fitted to the basic chassis for both home and overseas use, it was not until 1908 that progress demanded change. In 1908 the compound engine was vertically mounted behind the driver; a lay-out that claimed many advantages but neglected driver comfort, for he now had minimum protection from the weather.

The scope of the steam wagon can clearly be seen from this firm's catalogue for the period of the early 1920's. Included were tipping wagons; crane wagons; fuel tankers; street gully emptiers and even a steam bus, some of which saw regular service with the Grimsby Corporation Transport.

By 1925 the firm had attained technical excellence with their well known "W.G." series. Transmission was totally enclosed; power from the engine was transmitted to a dead rear axle through an intermediate differential casing and twin chains. Driver comfort had at last been taken into account with a totally enclosed cab. In addition to electric lighting, modern motor vehicle type controls were standard equipment.

Here then was another success story. Firms such as the Yorkshire Patent Steam Wagon Company; Leyland; Thorneycroft and Sentinel, had laid a foundation on which the heavy commercial vehicle industry of the future could be built. Yet, as is often the case, the price of progress means failure for some, and the steam wagon story is no exception. One such unfortunate was Jesse Ellis. If anyone should have flourished in the age of the steam wagon, it was this Maidstone man.

Already, at the age of 28, he was a successful businessman with a road contracting firm, a fleet of steam rollers, traction engines and steam cultivating tackle. The secret of his success appeared to be his uncanny ability to foresee future developments before his competitors.

With the coming of the 1896 Locomotive Act, Jesse Ellis decided to move into the building of steam wagons, having little doubt of the demand that would soon exist. To start this new venture, and carry on with his existing business, a new company was floated with an authorised capital of £60,000.

His initial design ideas were completely opposite to others who entered the field, being based on a patent granted on the 13th May, 1897. This was for a vehicle with vertical boiler and superheater placed to the rear, with a three cylinder radial engine over the back axle driving through chains to the rear wheels. Whether this design ever saw the light of day is open to debate. For at the 1898 Royal Show at Maidstone, the lorry he offered at a price of £450 was described as having the front mounted vertical boiler with undertype engine.

The business acumen of Ellis was never in doubt, for in a period when the fruit trade between Kent and London was increasing, he purposely advertised the wagon as ideal "for those engaged in the fruit trade", so bringing his lorry to the notice of a special section of the community. Ellis, however, did not restrict his vision to England but also produced a "Colonial Motor Buck Wagon" for use in Egypt and the Sudan. The reason for this was not hard to follow. His son, also called Jesse, was engaged in engineering work in the building of the Assuan Dam, and hence Jesse Ellis Snr. had first hand information of the requirements in the area.

For this model he reverted to the rear mounted boiler and engine. Sufficient commercial success came from it for Ellis himself to visit Egypt and consult and study the haulage needs of that country. Yet even this particular success could not bring the "buck", or rear mounted engined vehicle, to the fore in the commercial world, and soon Ellis himself had abandoned the idea completely and returned to the convential frontal lay-out.

Ellis was a perfectionist, and with every vehicle made he tried to eliminate all possible snags, and come forward with the best steam wagon on the market. Alas, in this he failed. With various models he tried different types of boiler, ranging from a vertical fire tube boiler to the then familiar locomotive type as used so successfully by other manufacturers. While his experiments may have seemed necessary, they failed to result in vehicles with a ready commercial market, with the result that the company began to spend more money than was coming in. Even so, Jesse Ellis came close to success. In his desperate search for perfection, he turned to the boiler making firm of T. Balmforth & Sons, and in collaboration with them produced the Ellis-Balmforth vertical firetube boiler. However, for all its design work, it remained an inefficient steamer.

Now he abandoned earlier experiments and turned to a form of boiler known as the "water tube" type, but still that elusive success evaded him. Despite the setbacks Jesse Ellis was not a man to be discouraged and by 1904 he was back with the "fire tube" type.

If he had but known it, this was a backward step. For his previous boilers had failed only from detail which caused steaming and cleaning troubles. If he had persevered just a little longer, then in all probability he would have overcome the faults and produced the type of vehicle he thought should have been built under the name of "Jesse Ellis". It was this inability to perfect what he considered the ultimate that led to his downfall. By 1904 the company were hard pressed for working capital, and a further issue of shares to a value of over two thousand pounds was authorised.

This financial crisis had an effect on future designs. Possibly against his

1930 Super Sentinel Steam Wagon, owned by the Ship's Company,
H.M.S. Sultan, Gosport, Hants

Another form of the Super Sentinel. This steam tractor was built in 1924 for use in heavy haulage

better judgement, but with the knowledge that money for further experimental work was scarce, Ellis turned to the locomotive boiler as used by Fodens and other makers. Then, again to save cost, he reverted from the successful "Ackermann" type of steering to a chain and bobbin form. This was another retrogade step. By 1906 half of the last share issue had been written off, and each £1 share held in the company had reduced in value by half. The urgent need was now to establish at least one model firmly in the minds of the buyers, and get a much needed injection of capital into the firm through commercial transactions.

At the time, however, with the exception of the larger manufacturers such as Foden, Leyland and Thorneycroft, steam wagons had a reputation for unreliability on long runs. Hence, smaller manufacturers such as Jesse Ellis were unable to corner a share of the market. The end came for him in April, 1907, when the affairs of the firm were put in the hands of the Official Receiver and Jesse Ellis, the man who had earlier proved his business ability beyond doubt, fell a victim to the steam age.

The causes of his trouble are hard to accurately pin-point. Possibly his first designs; when he dreamed of a rear powered wagon, were the first cause, for he was going against the conventional. But even this may have been averted if he had been satisfied to keep level with the technical developments of others, rather than aim for the ultimate which he was never able to achieve.

Despite the outcome of his dealings in steam wagons, Jesse Ellis can never be considered a failure. He showed the qualities that, in an age of the development of the engine, led to success. His desire to produce the perfect mechanical vehicle was the backbone on which British engineering later established a leading place in world trade. Jesse Ellis truly played his part in the story of steam.

While we can understand the failure of Ellis himself, in this age of a seemingly perpetual fuel crisis, many ask why the steam wagon, as it reached the perfection known in its later life, failed to compete with the new internal combustion engined vehicles. Without doubt, at the time of their decline, steam wagons had reached a peak of perfection that could have been the basis for future developments, to enable them to be carried through to the present day.

Sentinels have already been mentioned. Possibly their most famous challenger was the Foden range of undertypes. The "Speed Six", named after E. R. Foden's beloved Bentley, appeared in 1929. With a b.h.p. engine, mounted on pneumatic tyres, and capable of a speed of at least sixty miles per hour, it seemed that the future was still bright. Alas, as legislation had held back the development of steam on the road, so it was legislation that in many ways sounded its death knell. In their heyday steamers always held the advantage over petrol engined vehicles because, while petrol was heavily taxed, coal was not. Therefore steam wagons were cheaper to run.

Then came the 1933 Road Traffic Act. All forms of commercial vehicle taxation were overhauled, to give the internal combustion engine an equal chance against steam. The Road Fund Licence for steam vehicles was almost trebled while on diesels it was reduced, and made cheapest of all for petrol driven lorries.

Now steam wagons no longer held a financial advantage over their competitors, and men began to take notice of the disadvantages, among which were hot cabs, inadequate brakes and poor forward vision. So, almost overnight, the market collapsed and the internal combustion engine took the place of steam. But who knows what development could have done for the steam wagon, if the pros and cons of the two systems had been assessed by the buyer looking to the future. However, it was not to be, and yet one more chapter in the story of steam had closed.

CHAPTER IX

Steam Rollers

Possibly the best known of all steam engines is the humble steam roller. As a road-maker it found a way into town, village and hamlet. Indeed, wherever there was a pretention of a road surface, these rollers performed their task with an efficiency that was the hallmark of steam. Moving slowly backwards and forwards their ten tons or more total weight settled the road-making materials into a solid yet smooth surface suitable for every form of transport. In fact it is true to say that with the exception of the modern motorway network, every one of the roads owes its basic quality to the work of the steam roller.

Many firms made these rollers in one form or another, but without doubt the most famous came from the Rochester works of Thomas Aveling. Indeed whenever steam rollers are mentioned, most people automatically think of the "Rampant Horse" trademark that carried the name of the firm to the four corners of the world.

Aveling could not have chosen a more appropriate insignia. The "Rampant Horse", from the coat of arms of Kent, came originally from the banners of the invading war chiefs, Hengist and Horsa, who in A.D. 499 fought their way across the River Thanet into Kent. In like fashion, the products of Thomas Aveling had first to fight for supremacy in a market that attracted manufacturers by the hundreds in the early days of steam.

Even the word "Invicta", which graced the front of every Rochester creation, has an historical meaning that was not lost on Aveling. Signifying that the men of Kent, rather than risk defeat in battle with William the Conqueror, made their own peace, he in turn often found it necessary to make a strategic retreat when negotiating sales of his equipment in order to gain ultimate victory.

Aveling, of course, did not invent the roller. Who did is as unknown as the inventor of the wheel. Possibly the two may even be connected. For as the wheel developed from part of a tree trunk bred to take an axle, so the roller could have evolved from a similar system.

The rampant horse taken from the war banners of the invading chiefs Horsa and Hengist who, in AD 449 forced their way across the Thanet in Kent. Now the familiar trade mark of both Aveling and Porter and Aveling and Barford

Without doubt they were in use in earliest times, when circular stones were pulled by oxen and hand guided by extended axle shafts. In the Roman period similar devices were used, but more often than not with slaves substituted for oxen. The Romans must have found these primitive rollers efficient for the job, as they left us, on their withdrawal, with a road system without equal.

Unfortunately the thousand or so years after their evacuation saw it completely neglected and allowed to fade into total oblivion. In fact it was not until the 18th century, when men such as "Blind Jack" Metcalf of Knaresborough and General Wade in Scotland, came on the scene, that road building, as an art, was first discovered.

"Blind Jack" was indeed a remarkable man. Losing his sight when a boy, he soon proved that blindness was to be no handicap. He developed such a knowledge of the countryside of his native Yorkshire that long journeys on horseback held no terror for him. On one occasion he safely guided a stranger from York to Harrogate, skirting dangerous bog land where one false step could have brought death to both of them, in a manner that few men with sight could have achieved.

A 1907 Aveling and Porter Road Roller, in use until 1962

Small wonder that when road construction again came into prominence, "Blind Jack" proved himself the outstanding craftsman of the age. No terrain was too rough for him, for natural obstacles presented the kind of challenge that he enjoyed. His roads were outstanding examples of engineering skill, considering the primitive tools his men had for the task, and some even remain today. Although Jack Metcalf showed the way in which an effective road surface should be built, the general position at this time was one of inadequacy.

The Industrial Revolution saw traffic increase in quantity and weight, but the problem on a national scale, was delegated to local Turnpike Trusts. Although in many areas the Trusts did good work, their attitude on the whole was to fit traffic to roads rather than build roads to suit the traffic requirements. Early in the 19th century it seemed that the breakthrough had come. Telford and Macadam provided a network of roads that was the envy of the world. By 1820, the "golden age of the stage coach", road travel reached a scale never previously imagined. Three thousand stage coaches travelled the length and breadth of the country, employing more than thirty thousand men and one hundred and fifty thousand horses. All too soon, however, because of the advent of steam, it was over.

With the arrival of the railways, road travel dropped off. Road surfaces were allowed to fall into a state of disrepair and development stopped completely. Ironically, as steam caused this decay in the road system, so steam could not only have prevented it, but seen an even bigger growth in road transport. Yet the steam engine, as a form of mechanical transport on the roads, was burdened with such oppressive legislation that its development was impossible. In turn the railways were encouraged to prosper by those same people who saw steam in another form as an enemy to be fought at all costs.

Road repair now consisted of no more than the spreading of irregular shaped stones over the surface. Rolling was ignored; traffic using the roads would do that job itself in time. The effect on horses was terrible. The stones cut into their hooves and inflicted terrible suffering.

In such a restrictive atmosphere, Thomas Aveling grew up. When he first turned his thoughts to road rolling is not known. However, having to use these primitive roads to get produce to market from his farm at Ruckinge near the Romney Marshes, he saw the drawbacks at first hand and was well aware of the hardship caused.

It may be that his interest developed through the Rochester works he had established. Watching men dragging a cement filled iron cylinder to press stone into a smooth surface on the Rochester Esplanade in 1857, could have turned his thoughts to the use of a traction engine for the purpose.

Any ideas he had, however, had to be shelved for the time. His engine designs were being built for him by Clayton and Shuttleworth, the Lincoln firm, while devoted his efforts to establishing a production line of his own at the Rochester foundry. In fact, it was not until 1861 that the first traction engine was made at Rochester. Even then Aveling was preoccupied in further developments of that engine and the need to establish it commercially, so the appearance of his first "steam roller" was delayed until 1865.

It was not, however, a steam roller as we know it today. Aveling's first approach to the problem of road rolling was to have one of his standard traction engines towing a huge cast iron roller. The latter, made for him by an outside firm, weighed fifteen tons, was ten feet in diameter, and fitted with timber cross beams and a towing framework. To avoid turning the contraption round at the end of each pull, provision was made for the tow bar to be attached to the engine at either the front or back.

Primitive though it was, the roller found a market with the constructional firm of Easton, Amos and Anderson, who used it on roads in a park being built by them at Belvedere, Erith. Although the machine performed as

A 1930 Fowler Steam Roller

Aveling intended, he made a startling discovery while watching it at work. The actual roller was superfluous; weight transmitted by the wheels of the traction engine towing the roller was sufficient for the job in hand. So, with the knowledge that a light weight spread over a small area was better than a large weight over a large area, Aveling went back to the drawing board. The result was modifications to another of his 12 n.p.h. engines. Larger and wider wheels, with a diameter of seven feet and a width of three feet, were fitted, and new steering was designed.

Up to then, steerage was by the "pilot" system. A single fork mounted wheel in the horse shafts – a continuation from portable engine design – was turned in the direction of travel by a steersman seated on the device. Although it proved efficient for general purpose engines, when used for rolling purposes this single front wheel left an indentation in the road surface that the other wheels of this engine could not eradicate. So Aveling adopted the chain and pinion steering controlled by a ship's wheel. The roller, with a total weight of twenty tons, giving a ground pressure of three tons per

1923 Robey Tandem Road Roller

square foot, was put to work in London's Hyde Park, under contract to the Commissioner for Works, on the 1st December 1866.

The Illustrated London News of the period clearly showed the demand that existed for an efficient form of steam road roller: "The use of steam rollers for the crushing of stones and smoothing the surface of macadamised roads has long been advocated. Though we must wait for their general use, it is encouraging to see that the Commissioner of Her Majesty's Works has put one on trial in the parks".

Strangely enough, although the users and press alike reported favourably on the roller, Aveling appears to have lost all interest in it, for nowhere among the many records he left is there any mention of it. Instead, the year 1867 saw the introduction of what was to become a famous line in Rochester products, the "Liverpool Rollers". That the report in the Illustrated London News was not erroneous is proved by the edition of "Engineer" for the 22nd March, 1867. "Aveling", it said, "is to produce a steam road roller of 22 tons weight for work in Liverpool, and already nearly twenty other authorities have placed orders for similar machines".

These orders clearly showed Aveling the direction in which his firm had to progress, and from that time on, rollers above all other types of steam vehicle were his main concern. The "Liverpool Rollers" featured for the first time the two steering wheels joined together to roll the ground between the driving wheels. This was logical. What was not logical, and remains unexplained to this day, was the decision to reverse the layout of the roller, and bring the driving wheels to the front and the steering ones to the rear.

Whatever the reason, the design was a basic success. The Liverpool City Surveyor reported that for £1 per day running expenses, he not only had improved roads, but roads that could be more easily and cheaply cleaned. Orders flooded in and Aveling's only change in design was to reduce the weight from the original twenty-two tons, to a more efficient fifteen to twenty, so that the interlocking capacity of road stone would not be destroyed by crushing.

"Liverpool Rollers" were exported to France and India, and in 1868-9 became the first steam rollers in the United States of America. Their effectiveness is clearly shown by remarks of the Chief Engineer of Brooklyn, after two months of day and night working in Prospect Park: "One days rolling at a cost of ten dollars, gives the same results as two days rolling with the old seven ton roller, pulled by eight horses at a total cost of forty dollars".

One reason for the success of Aveling's machines was their large diameter wheels which truly rolled the ground, as opposed to the digging action of other maker's rollers with smaller wheels. Aveling, however, knew full well that this was only a temporary fault. Soon his rivals would increase the size of their wheels and his supremacy in the field would disappear.

*A 1947 Aveling and Barford roller, No. AG 760. The last
steam roller built for work in this country*

There were difficulties with the "Liverpool" range of rollers. Not only was it a poor hill climber, a feature the smaller designs of rivals improved on, and almost impossible to adapt to provide power for ancillary devices, but the reversed layout put heavy pressure on a factory geared to build conventional engines. He also had another worry. The brackets carrying the working parts were bolted directly to the boiler. Stresses distorted the holes through which the bolts passed, with a resultant corrosion and loss of steam.

His answer was the "hornplate" invention. By extending upwards the outside plates of the firebox, ideal support was provided for the working parts and all strain was removed from the boiler. This proved to be the basis for a completely new design which allowed him to revert to the conventional wheel arrangement, and also provided a lighter and cheaper roller than had previously been possible. The most striking feature of these 1871, 8 ton, 5 n.p.h. engines was the fitting of conical split rollers at the front. It was then erroneously thought that the resultant semi-skidding action assisted the ramming down of road stone, and that the stress placed on the axle and hub, by their natural tendency to run apart, left to right, was a small price to pay. Such was the reputation gained by this particular line, that at the Vienna Universal Exhibition of 1873, Aveling's rollers won the Order of Franz Joseph as the most outstanding exhibit in the show.

How many of this design were built is unfortunately not known, but at least two had a working life through into the early 1950's. Supplied new to the Corporation of Port of Spain, Trinidad, in 1876, one roller worked through almost continually until finally, when it could no longer provide an economic service, it went under the breaker's hammer. An inglorious end to a machine that was to prove the forerunner of the most famous rollers ever known.

Another example of the reliability of these Aveling rollers occurred in Norway, where roller No. 1457 joined the Oslo Municipal Road Department on the 19th July, 1878. The engine worked in and around the Norwegian capital until September, 1960. Still in good order, its retirement became necessary when its driver, after 42 years service, himself reached retirement age, and no young man could be found who was willing to be trained in the intricacies of steam.

A modern engine for this Marshall Roller, No. 86104 was made in 1931

This occasion, however, was not allowed to pass without due ceremony. The old Aveling, polished and shining and in a condition similar to the day it left the factory, was garlanded with flowers. Then, with the driver, Trygve Stromberg at the controls for the last time, and headed by the Municipal Brass Band and a guard of honour of road men who had worked with the roller during its long career, it set out from the Roads Department Headquarters to the Municipal Museum. There the Mayor of Oslo handed the old steamer into the care of the Curator of the Museum, and today it is the central attraction of the exhibits. A fitting retirement for this magnificent machine. It is a pity that the Port of Spain roller could not have received similar treatment.

Surprisingly, in view of their inherent drawbacks, conical split rollers were persevered with until 1879. Then asphalt from Trinadad's famous lake became more widely used as road-making material, and the conical shaped rollers proved to be completely inadequate in dealing with it. Their semi-skidding action pushed the asphalt in all directions and it was evident that survival, for Aveling, depended on a completely new front end for his machines.

The now famous cylindrical rolls were born, to be fitted as standard on all new machines, and as conversions, whenever required, to those originally equipped with split rollers. Other features also appeared at this time. Among them were the heavy rimmed solid flywheel, brought about because of the uproar from a horse-loving gentry, who believed the old spoked flywheel reflected sunlight into their animals' eyes and so caused them to bolt; geared transmission; and the practice of making the driving rolls slightly coned and of smaller inside diameter to compensate for wear over the width of the rollers.

This then was the steam roller that Aveling made famous throughout the world, for out of a total production of 12,700 engines at Rochester, over two thirds were steam rollers. Honours poured in. The Royal Agricultural Society of England awarded his rollers a silver medal, the only prize the Society ever gave to a steam roller. The French Exhibition at Beauvais brought in a gold medal, and both the Philadelphia International Exhibition of 1876 and the Paris International in 1878 gave their only awards ever made to steam rollers to Aveling's creations.

The year 1881 was to see further glory for Thomas Aveling. Prior to this, most of his engines had been single cylinder machines, but with some having two cylinders mounted in parallel. He well knew, however, that these engines lost in efficiency because of the impossibility of utilizing the energy of the steam to the full. Then, working as a contemporary of Fowler, he produced a compound cylinder machine exhibited at the Royal Show in 1881.

In the compound, the steam was first admitted to a high pressure cylinder, from which it emerged at a lower pressure, but nowhere near fully expended, and still containing energy that, in a single cylinder would go up the chimney. Now it was passed to a low pressure cylinder, to work another piston before being emitted into the smoke box. Thomas Aveling, unfortunately, did not live to see the results of this development, one of the most far reaching in the story of steam, and it was left to his successor, Thomas Lake Aveling, to perfect the compound.

Other makers, of course, were also active on the scene. Wallis and Stevens; Ruston; Burrell; Garrett; Fowler and Robey all produced some rollers, but the Rochester ones had almost a complete monopoly of the market.

While stone made up the material for road making, the heavy roller of the type exemplified by Thomas Aveling reigned supreme. When, however, asphalt took over completely, the position changed. On the hot tarmac, these heavy rollers tended to sink in at the end of each roll, so that a fast reversing engine was necessary to prevent damage to the road surface. Aveling's answer to this was the tandem roller which was fitted with full length rolls front and

A 1927 Berliner Maschinenbau A.G. single cylinder roller

rear and an engine designed so that it could be reversed without shutting off the steam – the prime cause of the reversing delay in the ordinary roller.

Robey of Lincoln was another firm who turned its attention to this type of roller, and the efficiency of their machines is shown by the fact that over twenty were bought by the Limmer and Trinidad Asphalt Company. A tribute indeed to their ability to work on the material for which they were designed. This firm even took the idea a step further with its tri-tandem, three of which were also sold to the same Trinidad firm for work on asphalt. These were based on the idea that three rolls arranged in tandem would eliminate the wave motion on the tarmac surface caused by conventional tandem rollers.

Another firm who also attained some degree of fame with road rollers was Wallis and Stevens, whose best design was introduced in 1924 at the Road Exhibition. The "Advance" model, as it was called, truly lived up to its name, being fitted with wide rear wheels of a similar diameter to the front ones, twin or duplex cylinders with their cranks at 90 degrees, thus doing away with the need for a flywheel, and almost instant reversing.

Today, when seen at Rallies, these old Wallis and Stevens rollers provide variety, in that they broke away from conventional design. In particular, the "Simplicity" range with their inclined boiler containing a replaceable firebox, never fail to draw the crowds.

It is, however, to Aveling's machines that this chapter is devoted, for only by following the works of one man can the growth and decline of steam be really appreciated. In decline, Aveling's machine proved almost as great as when that first primitive roller made its debut. Although many firms competed with Aveling in the field of roller production, no one at the Rochester firm eyed Barford and Perkins of Peterborough in that light. True, they were in the roller market, but their products were based on the internal combustion engine. To the old steam men, this could never surely replace the proven efficiency of steam in the field of heavy work.

William Barford became head of the Queen Street Engineering Works at Peterborough at about the same time as Thomas Aveling opened his works at Rochester. Then, Peterborough was concerned with the building of agricultural implements and horse drawn rollers. Although when Thomas Perkins joined the firm in 1872, initial experiments into the field of steam were considered, Barford and Perkins, when they turned their attention fully to rollers, worked almost exclusively on smaller models for use in parks, bowling greens and for landscape gardeners.

In fact, it was not until 1904, when the internal combustion engine became available that they decided to throw in their lot entirely with rollers to the exclusion of all other lines.

Both firms were progressing in the same chosen field, with Aveling

1901 Allchin Roller, No. 187

concentrating entirely on steam and Barford on the internal combustion engine. During the Great War both turned out rollers by the hundred for use on active service. The end of the war, however, saw Barford in a far better position than Aveling. The Peterborough design and construction methods were reasonably modern. At Rochester, the reverse was true. Their steam rollers had shown little variation, and worse, they relied completely on skilled craftsmen for their manufacture. Demand had increased, but the number of such men available had greatly decreased.

The Rochester works were reorganised to make extensive use of jigs and as many parts as possible were prefabricated for standardisation. To accommodate the new system, a range of nineteen steam rollers, between six and twenty tons, made a clean sweep of all previous models. Design changes were inevitable. The slide valve disappeared to make way for the piston valve, which needed less skill to make and fit. Rollers with reversible rims and brushes were made identical so they could be changed from side to side to equate wear.

By 1921, Thomas Lake Aveling saw that individual progress could be difficult, and twelve firms, including Barford's of Peterborough, joined in an association called Agricultural Engineers Ltd., to standardise marketing and other techniques. Although each firm retained its own identity, the wind of change was gradually sweeping Rochester and Peterborough closer together. The world economic depression had an effect on both firms. Short time became standard. Men were laid off and vast areas of the Rochester factory stood empty. Although competitors in many ways, both Aveling and Barford relied on the same type of market. The formation of Aveling and Barford and Perkins (Sales) Ltd., in 1928, was a logical step.

With the death of Thomas Lake Aveling in 1931 the end appeared to be in sight for the Rochester works. Consideration was given to Barford's moving moving lock, stock and barrel to Kent, but before details could be finalised, the A.G.E. group collapsed. The Official Receiver was called in, and only the financial genius of Edward Barford saved the two firms from extinction.

So, like a Phoenix rising from the ashes. Aveling and Barford was formed from the debris of the separate firms, and today their position as producers of the world's largest rollers stands unassailable.

For some time steam rollers were made side by side with the Barford designed internal combustion engine roller, but alas it could not last. Steam was on the way out but, of all forms of actual steam road vehicle, the steam roller can be said to have been the last to fall, with the final model rolling off the production line as late as 1947. Today the accent is on the diesel engine.

But Thomas Aveling would be proud if he could see the progress that has resulted from that first humble roller towed behind an equally primitive traction engine, the forerunner to an assembly line whose products are known and respected throughout the world.

CHAPTER X

Fairground Organs and Miniature Engines

On many occasions, the thrill of the Rally is experienced even before the meeting is reached. These, of course, are the times when the still, summer air carries the faint but unmistakable sound that means but one thing - the fairground organ.

Today there are few steam gatherings without at least one example of these old instruments that are associated, in the minds of all, with fun, gaiety and enjoyment. They have an appeal all their own, and many enthusiasts spend their spare time preserving and restoring them to add glamour and excitement to the proceedings.

The popularity of the tunes that have survived the various musical fads is evident, not only from those patiently standing in the vicinity with portable tape recorders, picking up both the atmosphere and sound of the old steam fairs, but also from the fairground and street organ records that are displayed for sale wherever steam gives us an excuse to gather at the shrine of nostalgia.

Organs, of course, fall into various classes. There are the church and cathedral organs, and, now unfortunately another victim of the march of progress, the cinema organ. These all had one particular thing in common; they required an organist to play them. The fairground, though, makes no such requirement, being operated by perforated cards. They originated on the continent around 1870, with the undisputed best being the work of that famous name in the organ world, Gavioli.

The fairground organ has altered little during its hundred or so years of life, and was the logical successor to the old "barrel organ", that mechanical instrument pushed along while the operator turned the handle to produce fascinating music.

Possibly one of the great attractions of the organ is the fact that almost every instrument can be reproduced on it, be it oboe, or bassoon, trombone or trumpet. Indeed, those heavily carved Gavioli Orchestrophones, with their total of 110 keys, could replace a full band of musicians.

The fundamental difference between the fairground organ and its brothers in religious houses and cinemas, is that on the former there are no keys on show. They are operated by a book of hinged and folded punch cards. The accuracy and thoroughness required of these cards is illustrated by the fact that even in the early 1930's they could cost the organ owner anything up to twenty five pounds. Each is punched for a particular type of organ, having a set number of keys and registers.

In use, the music book is fed into rollers by the operator, and from then on until the end of the music everything is done automatically. The keys, initially, are all depressed by the insertion of the punch card and it is the holes, which allow the keys to rise, that control the melody. The same punch card also controls the drums and cymbals and the moving figures fitted to the front of the organ.

To the showman, they were a boon, providing musical accompaniment for the rides yet requiring little attention from the man himself. And as an added bonus their repertoire was extensive, covering the works of Bach, popular songs, marches and the famous classics. During their lifetime many of the organs attained a mystique equalled only by the engines that today accom-

A fairground organ, "Ceol", powered by a traction engine model

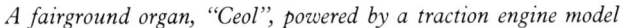

pany them on their public appearances. One seen regularly at Rallies even has the doubtful honour of being the organ used in a much discussed incident, when the organist was shot dead by invading German troops during World War II for refusing to stop playing the Belgian National Anthem.

Possibly one of the most attractive fairground organs to visit the Rally scene is a beautifully restored Chiappa organ, "Ceol". This started its working life on the cakewalk of a travelling showman, then moved into the hands of a Scottish operator before crossing the sea to Ireland. At the end of World War II it was cast aside as scrap. Fortunately, it came into the hands of a preservationist and today has been restored to its original condition.

However, as beautiful as the organ itself is, what proves to be a fascinating attraction with most attenders is the steam engine that provides the motive power. Here is no great Showman's Road locomotive of yester-year, but rather an accurately detailed model "Burrell" traction engine. "Prince" is indeed a tribute to the ultimate in the scale builders art, and a fitting introduction to yet another aspect of the Rally movement, miniature engines.

Miniatures, for these smaller examples deserve more than the title

A Fowler ploughing engine built from drawings of an
1894 Model T.1 double drum ploughing engine

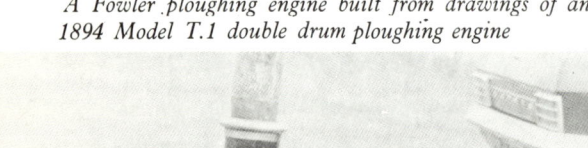

"model", have a definite part to play in the preservation movement. In the beginning owners of full size restored steamers, tended to cast such reproductions to one side, as if unworthy of the attention of the enthusiast. Yet today their worth is well recognised, with some organisers getting together steam meetings solely for the benefit of the smaller exhibits, prohibiting all but one or two full size engines. In many ways, this is as it should be. For although many of the original working traction engines have been lost forever, through the art of the engineers who devote their time and effort to building miniatures, we can again see them at first hand.

One example of this is to be seen in the Science Museum, London, where a model of Usher's rotary cultivator of 1849 is on display. This however, is a model with a difference, for it dates from the year of the full size machine's manufacture, and was used for advertising purposes. The maker had no alternative, if he wished the world at large to know of his latest developments, than to insert a small advertisement in a newspaper. Photographs, as we know

Miniature Burrell engine, "Prince", capable of driving
a fairground organ for nine hours

them today, were then unknown, and the moving of a full scale engine from place to place presented many difficulties.

Models were made and taken to the prospective customers to demonstrate the main points of the machine being offered. As with their full size counterparts, most of these "travellers samples" have been lost forever, but those that have survived provide an accurate means of following industrial development in this country.

In the same way, models made by enthusiasts in our own time provide a similar service. With the passing of the years, many old steamers are gone for good, remembered only by the makers' catalogues and drawings and plans that have survived.

No better example of this exists than the 1894 Fowler double drum ploughing engines. No originals remain, but through the patience of miniature engineers at least one such engine graces the Rally field. "Pamela", as this Fowler is affectionately called, is a perfect scale miniature of a Fowler double drum ploughing engine, made from plans and blueprints supplied by the firm themselves. Here we have the chance to see, in reduced scale, an engine that played a notable part in the development of steam cultivation. Without it we should have to rely solely on the written word and sales catalogues for descriptions of this remarkable type of engine.

Model building, of course, is no place for the man without patience, or the person who wants to see a quick return for his labours. "Prince", for example, took 3,000 hours to build, but the results are as impressive as any full size engine. Standing 45″ high and tipping the scales at one ton, the engine can pull five times its own weight on level ground, drive a circular saw, or generate electricity. So reliable is it that on many occasions it has driven its companion organ, "Ceol", for periods of up to nine hours, steaming, in the process, through one hundredweight of coal and 25 gallons of water.

Yet "Prince" could be said to have been a "quick build" compared with the work of a Cornwall builder who spent no less than 7,000 hours in the construction of a magnificent Burrell Showman's Road locomotive. So painstaking is the detail on this miniature that it has a crane and working dynamo. Other impressive specifications include compound cylinders, three speed compensating gear, winch drum and working flywheel and rear wheel brakes.

Often these miniatures find themselves modified from the original, just as full size engines are themselves altered or adapted. Only recently, following the publication of a photograph, I had a letter from an old time builder who signed himself with the charming title of Engineer and Millwright, telling how he himself had started work on the engine that was the subject of the illustration. It was designed, detailed and made in his own private works in 1940. What proved impossible with the facilities that the builder had

An example of the model builders' art. A Showman's three speed Road Locomotive started originally as a one-third size Fowler General Purpose engine

A detailed example of a Fowler ploughing engine, one of an identical pair

available at his works, was done during periods of firewatching at Saxon's Big Engine Works at Stretford Lancs. However, before the work was completed circumstances forced a sale of the miniature.

A list of the parts at the time of sale shows without doubt the work and thoroughness that goes into each such engine. Included in the sale was a full set of drawings which, according to the builder, constituted a work of art, together with a set of sketches of parts, all the patterns, tools, gauges, templates, the wheel building jig, back axle, drum differential gear, ring final drive, axle boxes, springs, guides, hornplates, blacks stay, tender plates etc, boiler, tubes, seatings, boiler mountings, chimney, smoke box and pipework. Also included were all machine cut steel gearing for 3 speed, 4 shaft drive with rise and fall mechanism. Although the front and rear wheels were not built up, the rings, spokes, hubs and bushes were complete. Originally it was planned as a one-third size scale Fowler General Purpose engine, but in its later construction a dynamo and canopy were added, and today it represents a truly beautiful Showman's Road locomotive.

Although it may be thought that only trained engineers would even attempt

A scale model of a Wallis and Stevens steam roller

One of the many models to be seen at Traction Engine Rallies

An example of the dedication that the model builder will devote to his art

the seemingly mammoth task of building one of these old giants of steam in miniature, this is not always the case. One seen regularly at Rallies, was built and is owned by a man who had never tackled engineering construction in his life and who makes a living through working in wood.

Today, as interest spreads, so Societies are being formed to take the beginner through the intricacies of engineering practice, bringing together those with a desire for such work but without the necessary knowledge. Their efforts must be appreciated by all.

In the miniature section will be found old Fowler Ploughing engines, Showman's Road locomotives in all their glory, the humble portable, steam rollers of every description, as well as beautiful steam wagons and other road vehicles. Those who give these smaller engines but a cursory glance at Traction Engine Rallies are truly missing out on a great deal of enjoyment.

These then are some of the delights that meet the eye at Rallies, but there others that take us back in time to the age when steam reigned supreme, some of the most fascinating being the old steam fire engines.

Here was steam with a difference, for on show are examples of engines that were not fully powered by steam, relying on the horse for motive power, and

The intricate work which the model maker can build into his engine is clearly shown by this freelance general purpose traction engine

steam for the operation of the fire pumps. What marvellous machines they were, and what problems they set their designers.

Take for example the old 1908 Merryweather steam fire pump, owned by a Nottinghamshire enthusiast and a welcome visitor to most Midland steam meetings. The "Greenwich Gem", as the makers called her, was pulled by two horses side by side, which immediately raised problems. The designers had to come up with an engine that could raise steam quickly and continuously and yet still be within a weight limit that would not impose hardship on the horses between the shafts. To overcome these difficulties the firm designed a special boiler of the semi-flash type of thin steel plate. So efficient was it that it could get up steam from cold in eleven minutes, and in a remarkable three minutes if warm water was used. Another problem concerned the water supply itself. Because of the weight problem, a large tank of water could not be carried and so a small supply adequate only to let the engine commence work immediately on arrival was provided. Once at the scene it would pump from any convenient source. But that small water supply on the engine meant the fireman in charge had to judge things very finely indeed. Woe betide a man who lit his fire too early so that all the feed water was exhausted when the brigade arrived at the blaze. All this, however, adds to the interest of the engines, and machines such as these old fire pumps well deserve their place in the rally field.

Another minority group are the old crane engines – massive road locomotives fitted with a steam crane at the rear so that they provided a means of both haulage and lifting power. Many of these engines were employed in the field of heavy engineering, when manufactured goods such as heavy boilers were moved.

How useful these steamers must have proved with the means to lift the load onto its tender, provide the haulage or part of the haulage power during transit, and then be used to lift and move the heavy load at its destination. Unlike normal heavy road locomotives these cranes need not stand idle between journeys, but found many uses in and around the engineering yards where lifting power was needed.

So steam traction engines gave England every form of transport it required, and on many occasions the uses found for them were far from those intended

The Merryweather, "Little Gem", Fire Pump

The "cockpit" of the Merryweather Fire Engine

Fowler "Super Lion" Crane engine, built in 1929

by the maker. In Lincolnshire, when the power failed at a newspaper office, the services of a local traction engine owner were obtained, and soon the presses were again rolling as the old engine stood outside, happily chuffing away with the drive belt passed through an open window to the printing machines. Even more remarkable, in the Derbyshire village of Barlow a very unorthodox use was found for a traction engine, Here, on the occasion of every Royal celebration such as a coronation or a jubilee, one of the engines owned by the Morgan family of Barlow was used to brew the tea that formed an essential part of the village celebrations.

Many of those who tasted the brew insisted that the connoisseur could distinguish between the tea from a Fowler and that from a Burrell. An interesting reflection of this old village custom is that when Barlow held its Silver Jubilee party in 1935, the Marshall engine that added the final touch to the refreshments had itself celebrated its Golden Jubilee the previous year.

Such is the history that these engines have built around themselves.

CHAPTER XI

Steam Cars, Motor Cycles and Aircraft

The traction engine was the success story of the age of steam, but it was not solely to the development of these iron giants that our ancestors turned their attentions. Steam was the only real form of motive power that they knew, and their ambitions were no less than ours, and steam was envisaged as a means of propulsion for everything from motor cycles to aircraft.

In this modern age, as jet powered aircraft soar through the sky at supersonic speeds, these old ideals may seem primitive and basic, but remembering the first crude attempt to harness steam for the benefit of the agriculturalist, one can only wonder what would have happened if they had continued with their developments.

Although these ideas have perished with the passing of time and those concerned with them, in no way can they really be called failures. As man works to develop an idea, so inevitably some of those ideas will prove to be beyond either his capabilities or the capabilities of the medium in which he has chosen to work. In the story of the day to day life during that period, experiments that went wrong have an equal pride of place with the success stories. In no way could it be said that the work of these early visionaries was wasted, for the very first motor cycle that the world saw was, in fact, a steam model. This great event took place in Winthrop, Massachusetts, U.S.A., when a certain W. W. Austin astounded his neighbours by appearing on the roads on a crude, steam powered two wheeled device. Contemporary to Austin's work were the experiments of Monsieur Perreaux in France, who produced his masterpiece in December, 1868.

It is the Austin velocipede, however, that laid the foundation for future development and, from writings of the time, we have a fairly clear picture of what this first motor cycle looked like. It had a twin cylinder engine, with the two cylinders being fitted one either side of the main stay of the frame. The piston rods drove direct to cranks fitted to the rear wheel axle, with the coal fired boiler slung midway between the wheels. The chimney, necessary to direct away the smoke, was brought round so that it came up at the rear of the saddle. Primitive it may have been, but its maker claimed to have ridden it for some 2,200 miles without any breakdown or mishap.

If this was the case, he was more fortunate than a Glasgow enthusiast, James Sadler, who in 1926 began to develop his own form of a steam powered two wheel vehicle. His experiments could hardly claim to have been a total success.

In the first place his ideas were based on a water tube boiler and twin cylinder engine. The dangers of this type of machine are evident from reports that he lost four pairs of trousers through them bursting into flames as he manoeuvred his machine along the roads and lanes. As well as this he is reported to have suffered severe body burns, while unfortunate spectators, standing too close to the cycle's flues, lost their eyebrows. Small wonder that he decided his ideas were not really practicable.

Despite his injuries, this stalwart inventor did not give up; rather did he turn his mind to the possibility of sidecar outfits. However, insurance companies showed a definite lack of enthusiasm when the question of cover

A 1904 Allchin General Purpose engine, No. 1499, "Evedon Lad"

for road use was raised, and reluctantly this able Scot had to turn his attentions to other fields.

Sadler's trials and tribulations were however still to come when Austin proudly introduced his design to an astounded public. Austin's ideas led to development work by other enthusiasts, including one Lucius D. Copeland, who in 1881 fitted a steam engine to a standard cycle, but with a different approach to Austin.

It was not intended to provide a form of continuous motive power but rather power that could assist the cyclist when travelling up hills and steep gradients. This idea, however, had to be dropped as it proved to be too dangerous and hazardous.

Copeland's next attempt was more successful. A lightweight steam engine, weighing no more than 19lbs, was fitted to a bicycle and provided sufficient power to drive it at 12 m.p.h. Now he searched for others with equal faith in the future of the steam driven two wheeler, who were prepared to put up the necessary capital to found a works for production.

Inevitably, his search was hard and long, but by 1887 he succeeded in obtaining the good offices of financier Sanford Northrop and two others. The Northrop Manufacturing Company was formed in the American city of Camden, New Jersey and soon a steam propelled tricycle was coming off the production line. Such was its efficiency that the designer regularly made journies of over 150 miles without much trouble.

Next to leave the factory was a steam cycle based on the idea of the safety cycle, and it is interesting to recall that the later addition of an extra wheel at the side on which a passenger seat was fitted was the forerunner of the motor cycle combination which later proved so popular.

By 1890 Copeland had developed a machine that not only carried sufficient water for a thirty mile journey, but one that could be started up from cold in five minutes, and attain the then great speed of ten m.p.h.

However, doubts about the financial viability of the firm grew in Copeland's mind. He became convinced that it was impossible to build these steam cycles to the required standard at a price the public would pay and so, unfortunately, he disappeared from the arena.

Others, however, did not share this feeling of gloom, and in France several fairly successful models made their appearance. Towards the end of the 19th century, sad to say, the introduction of the De Dion petrol engine drove the idea of a successful and commercial light steam engine from the minds of most manufacturers, although amateur enthusiasts in many countries continued to experiment.

Surprisingly enough, experiments in England began in 1910 by Pearson and Cox, who had successfully been building light steam cars for some years. By 1912 they had a design on the market that could, in the words of those who tested it, travel at 40 miles per hour, was a good hill climber, and retailed for approximately £40.

However, two years later Europe was plunged into the horror of the Great War, and all thoughts of the steam bicycle passed from the minds of designers and public alike.

The period of the war was one from which this form of travel was never to recover. Only those such as Sadler, with an inbuilt love of steam, even considered the possibility in the post war years. So another use for steam disappeared before it really began.

While the practicality of steam as a form of power for two wheeled vehicles is apparent to us all, its use as a means of aerial travel is not so logical, yet that is exactly what our ancestors envisaged.

The thought of flight, of Man being able to take to the air in the manner of the birds, has of course always attracted man, and through the centuries various ideas and experiments were tried out. With these thoughts in the minds of so many, it is not unreasonable that enthusiasts of the steam age should give serious consideration to air travel powered by that locomotive force that had served so well in other fields.

Surprisingly a lot of the basic ideas were later proved by our own engineering abilities and technical knowledge to be sound. The very first attempt came in the 1830's when a model with flapping wings, imitating the action of birds, was demonstrated in England. The "wings" flapped as planned but unfortunately the machine suddenly blew up, and another idea had entered the long list of failures.

From this, however, came the idea of the rotating blades fitted above the body of the machine; an idea that, through our helicopters, we now know is perfectly practicable.

One of the most ambitious designers in the field of aeronautics was, without doubt, William Henson, who, by 1842 had outlined his specifications for an "Aerial Steam Carriage". His design included many features that later proved requisites of all aircraft design, but he had no engine to power it. He knew that steam was the only possible means, but the engines were too heavy and cumbersome. So, in partnership with a close friend John Stringfellow, he set up a company to work on the development of a light yet powerful engine suitable for air transportation.

The best they could accomplish was a 20 ft. wing span model powered by a small steam engine, and this could only travel along guide rails and then glide to safely to the ground as it came off the inclined end of the rails.

After this, Stringfellow left the partnership, but Henson continued with his work. At the Aeronautical Exhibition held at the Crystal Palace in 1868, he was awarded a prize of £100 for a light but durable engine powering a model on the triplane principle. Regretably, however, this turned out to be Henson's swan song. Although he tried with further ideas, none of them came into being as actual flying machines, yet his contribution to the design of a light steam engine has long been acknowledged.

In France, steam flight was approached from a different direction with steam engines powering lighter air ships. In 1852 Henri Giffard became the first man to fly by means of steam power.

On the 24th September of that year he became airborne in Paris and travelled seventeen miles on a platform containing a steam engine driving a propeller supported by an 80,000 cubic feet gas bag. These experiments, however, were also doomed to failure when it was discovered that hot steam and inflammable gasses did not combine safely.

The honour of being the first man to fly in a steam powered aeroplane fell to another Frenchman. Felix du Temple de la Croix had been experimenting for many years in this field and in 1874, on the outskirts of Brest, he demonstrated his latest accomplishment, a monoplane powered by a high pressure steam engine and piloted by a naval acquaintance of the inventor.

In front of a fascinated crowd the aeroplane was pushed onto an inclined ramp and the engine lit. Suddenly the craft began to move and as it left the end of the ramp a cheer went up as, for a short distance, the machine was actually airborne. The distance of the flight was negligible, being more a powered hop than a flight in the true sense of the word, but in the 19th century it was a landmark in the story of aviation and acted as encouragement to others.

Gradually, from that date, steam powered aeroplanes began to attract the attention of an enthralled public as more and more demonstrated that basically, flight was possible. True, these were mere powered glides of distances under 200 yards, but they did show, that even if steam was not the solution, man had begun to conquer the air.

There was a long way to go yet, but early pioneers such as Sir Hiram Maxim, of machine-gun fame, gave encouragement to those who were later to follow in their footsteps.

Maxim was already established and respected as an inventor when he turned his attentions to aerial travel. To business acquaintances who asked his opinion of Man's ability to conquer the air, he replied that "at least £100,000 and five years work would be needed". In typical fashion, when his backers gave the go ahead, he approached his task with a period of intensive study of earlier work. All forms of design, wings, propellers, and thrust developed by the available engines, were recorded by Maxim and the results used to produce, initially, captive models that were demonstrated on tracks which allowed them to actually leave the ground but prevented uncontrolled flight.

From the visual effects of these, and measured data, he made his first true aeroplane. For power he turned to the two compound steam engines developing 350 h.p. each and driving a propeller of 17 feet diameter.

The first tests were again conducted on rails. A railway of the normal type was laid for a distance of some third of a mile, on which the aeroplane's wheels were fitted. Above this was another rail, this time inverted so that the flanged wheels would fit into it as the 'plane lifted. By this means measurements could be made of the thrust if the aircraft effected a lift from the ground under steam power, without any of the inherent dangers that could have resulted if it had been tested in normal free flight.

The 31st July, 1894, saw history in the making. On the first runs the aeroplane failed to lift from the lower rails, but, as pressure was increased until the propellers were turning at some 500 r.p.m., the craft lifted fully from the bottom rail and its wheels were engaged with the top rail within 600 feet. Such was the thrust available that the rail proved incapable of holding the steaming monster and within 1,000 yards it had broken loose. If the steam had not been turned off it would have pulled its nose upwards to the skies.

Success seemed inevitable after this. The work of Maxim seemed to have carried the idea of a steam driven aeroplane further than any others, to the verge of a breakthrough.

'Yet, on the edge of success, he abandoned his experimental work. Instead of strengthening the weak points in the airframe itself, shown up during that famous rail ride, Sir Hiram Maxim turned his back on aeronautics and devoted his attentions elsewhere. His reasons, although inexplicable to those concerned with the future of steam flight, are easy to understand. Until then the cost of experiments had amounted to almost a quarter of a million pounds. Much more would be needed for eventual success, and furthermore the lease had expired on the premises he was using.

However, it cannot truly be said that steam had added yet another chapter to its story of failures. Although steam could never be as efficient as the internal combustion engine when used for powering Man's attempts at flight, other successes did follow.

In the middle 1930's the Besler Brothers in California fitted a steam engine to a conventional light aircraft which was then successfully flown by William Besler at many meetings and airshows. So, in actual fact, steam eventually proved that it could be used, and had it received the same development programme that we have given to the internal combustion engine, who knows just what position it could have held today.

Truly, steam marks one of the most epic periods in our history and, from those first humble portable engines, through the magic of the traction engine at its peak, steam lorries, cars, and motor cycles, and even aircraft, it lives on today. Through the patient work of the enthusiast we can sample and enjoy this great period from the past, by leaving home, with the family any summer weekend, and visiting a Steam Rally.

Index